Praise for *Wait, How Do I Lead My Team?*

"Wait, How Do I Lead My Team? is valuable for business professionals at any age. The writing templates are easy to follow and full of practical tips. It's a must-have item on any leader's desk!"

— Shannon Kendrick
Director of strategic partnerships and
intergovernmental affairs, U.S. Peace Corps

"Wait, How Do I Lead My Team? is a well-organized manual of practical reminders and insightful suggestions perfect for communication challenges and opportunities we all face as business leaders. You will want this resource close at hand."

— Gary Plaag
Adjunct Faculty, Raymond A. Mason School of Business
at the College of William & Mary

"The book is user friendly, engaging and stated in common language without complicated jargon. This is a perfect read for teachers and students alike!"

— Regina Morrone
Career and technical education (CTE) program manager
for Family & Consumer Sciences, Fairfax (Va) County Public Schools

"Another great read from Danny Rubin! Whether you're building a team, running a large operation or leading an on-campus organization, this book is for you!"

— Joshua Sushan
Director of leadership development,
Alpha Epsilon Pi Fraternity

"Danny Rubin tackles the seemingly ordinary emails and routine conversations that confront a leader day after day. He then provides simple strategies that leave a lasting impression."

— Jay Reid
Sr. Director, Football Operations Technology Strategy,
National Football League

"While I was reading, I often found myself screa
seen many of these mistakes come from colleague
and the gaffes do discredit them. I recommend
to be taken seriously and gain respect from the

Editor-in-Chief, Coastal Virginia Magazine / CoVa biz

Wait, How Do I Lead My Team?

Inspiring Templates for Interoffice Emails, Client Outreach, Presentations & More

Danny Rubin

For information about this title or to order books and/or electronic
media, contact the publisher at www.dannyhrubin.com.

Library of Congress Control Number: 2018914661

ISBN: 978-0-9963499-8-7 (Print)
978-0-9963499-9-4 (Ebook)

Printed in the United States of America

Cover design: Paul McCarthy

Interior design: 1106 Design

TO EVERYONE WHO KNOWS THEY ARE DESTINED TO LEAD,
THIS BOOK IS FOR YOU.

Introduction

When you're in charge, you're always under a microscope.

Employees and other stakeholders watch your every action and hold you to the highest standards.

You're a leader. What did you expect?

That's why leaders (or people who aspire to hold the title) must treat their communication skills with great care.

A single email to your team is more than a one-off message; it's a window into your management style.

A monthly check-in meeting with a client is bigger than a routine appointment; it's an open display of how you handle business relationships.

In my first book, *Wait, How Do I Write This Email?*, we explored writing and speaking for job seekers.

Then in *Wait, How Do I Promote My Business?*, we examined the best ways to spread the word about our products and services.

Now, we turn to leadership. That's because, in every phase of our professional lives, communication skills either drive us forward or hold us back.

That reality goes for leaders in a student organization all the way up to veteran CEOs.

In *Wait, How Do I Lead My Team?*, we break down challenges in management, client relations, networking, giving presentations and more — always with a focus on the **how.**

How should we write and speak in a way that makes people say, "Now *that's* what a leader looks like"?

After all, life under a microscope does have an upside.

If you conduct yourself just right, then you — and your reputation — will be larger than life.

CONTENTS

Author notes

Before you begin, two points about the book:

1. I use the lessons and templates in the book for workshops and as part of classroom instruction. They are the foundation of everything I teach. While I know strong communication skills can boost your leadership style, I don't guarantee my techniques will lead to new relationships, deals or revenue. I *can* help you earn the respect of clients and colleagues, and that's a great place to start.
2. Every person, school, business and organization I name in the book are fictitious.

Chapter 1
Writing Master Class for Leaders

Classic Writing Fails

NUMBERS

In the end, leadership is a numbers game.

Here, I don't refer to the company's bottom line but rather how you write numbers in emails and documents.

Yes, the actual use of numbers.

To be grammatically correct, you spell out the numbers 0-9. As in, "This month, we added three new clients."

For 10 and higher, you use the number itself. As in, "This month, we added 12 new clients."

It's subtle, yes. But you are the leader, and your words carry weight. Sloppy grammar undercuts your influence.

Keep an eye on the numbers in your writing and make sure you follow the guideline. It's the little stuff that makes the biggest difference.

CAPITALIZATION

If you take a quick scan of the chatter on social media, you will spy the lawless world of capitalization.

People capitalize whatever words they so choose. There are no rules or order.

EXAMPLE:

> "I'm so Excited to begin my New Job on Monday. I will be the Regional Manager at Acme Corporation and oversee two District Offices. Can't Wait!"

Only three words in the sentences above should be capitalized (aside from the first word in each sentence). Do you know what they are?

Acme Corporation and **Monday.**

Why? The trio are proper nouns. Let's break down the other capitalized words and why they should be lower case.

- **Excited** — We don't capitalize words based on our emotions.

- **New Job** — Again, I'm happy you're in good spirits, but we don't capitalize words because they feel special. Only proper nouns.

- **Regional Manager** — It's a common misconception, but we only capitalize job titles when they precede our name (Ex: Regional Manager Alan Moore versus Alan Moore, a regional manager...).

- **District Offices** — Again, not proper nouns. If the building is called the Helen Summers Regional Multiplex, then yes, capitalize all the livelong day. Do you see the difference?

- **Can't Wait!** — You already know what I'm going to say.

As a leader, writing is paramount. When done well, it commands respect from employees and clients. Capitalization plays a huge role because it's a factor in every sentence you write.

Keep this idea close: 90% of the time, the word you **want** to capitalize should instead be lower case.

Save the capitalization for the words that deserve the treatment.

People will notice.

WITH "I" OR "ME"?

Grammar is tough, and sometimes we understand the rules but not *all the way.*

Here's a classic example: The boss, John, stands up to speak to his team and says, "I want to update everyone on the conversation between Tina and I."

Sigh. There's nothing worse than looking foolish while you *try* to appear smart.

To John's credit, he knew he shouldn't say "...between me and Tina." That's a no-go right from the start. "Me and Tina" isn't correct; many people in the business world know that one.

To say the phrase properly, John thought it should be "...between Tina and I." But that's where he and so many other leaders and managers are wrong. And in doing so, they lose respect from employees who know the right way to say the line.

What *is* the answer?

It's "between Tina and me." When we use a prepositional phrase, we need to use an indirect pronoun (ex: "me") instead of a direct one ("I"). Look, I don't make the rules. I just follow them.

Other options could be:

- ▸ "**for** Tina and me"

- ▸ "**from** Tina and me"

- ▸ "**with** Tina and me"

There are a lot of prepositional phrases. You can google it.

The "you and I/you and me" rule is tricky because we must think about the correct phrase as we're talking. There's no time to pause and play it out in our heads.

Still, when you say something like, "between Tina and I," it can hurt your reputation within the management ranks and in front of your employees. People may think, "He's in charge, but he's not that smart." You don't want to enter that territory.

In so many ways, proper writing and speaking engenders respect from all corners of the office.

"Between you and me" is a little phrase that gives a major boost to your management style.

"-ING" WORDS

1. All week, our group **has been analyzing** data, **preparing** a report and **practicing** the pitch to investors.

2. All week, our group has **analyzed** data, **prepared** a report and **practiced** the pitch to investors.

Which sentence comes across more direct and assertive?

If you said sentence #2, you are correct. When we drop the "-ing" from our words, the sentences become shorter and the tone is more confident.

As you finish emails and documents, use the search function and look for "ing." You will be surprised how often the three little letters find their way into our writing.

Each time, "ing" slows down the pace and undercuts our effectiveness as both a communicator and a leader.

If you want people to respect your leadership style, cut out "ing." The letters are **doing** nothing but **holding** you back.

Let me try the last line again.

The letters **do** nothing but **hold** you back.

See my point?

LEAD WITH "WE"

Leadership doesn't mean go ahead and **take all the credit**.

If employees observe leaders drop a lot of, "I did this" and "I did that" and, in essence, "look at me go!", the word choice can create unnecessary distance and fracture the relationship between management and staff.

If you, as a team leader, **did** accomplish a task, then it may be appropriate to lead with "I."

For example, in an email to multiple staff members: "I went ahead and called our client, Morgan, to reschedule the meeting for Friday at 2:30 p.m."

But if the particular action involved several hands, then don't act like you did all the heavy lifting — or omit the people who played a key role.

Here's an email to multiple staff members, several who could have helped with the "heavy lifting."

"Thanks to **everyone** who put in the extra hours over the weekend to finish out the RFP for the Jackson account. That's an account **we'd** love to have to build up our robotics division."

Now, observe how much differently that quote reads with a focus on "I."

"Good news. The RFP for the Jackson account is done and submitted. **I** hope we land the account because **I'd** love to add that project to the company's robotics division."

Feel a different vibe here? All about me, me, me — the great and esteemed company leader.

Keep an eye on your "I" usage. Your employees sure will.

Smooth, Polished Writing

SEVEN WRITING MISTAKES LEADERS NEVER MAKE

Employees, clients and others in the business community hold leaders to the highest standards. Margin for error: zero.

That's why you need to watch out for classic writing mistakes. Here are the seven biggest ones.

1. It's definitely, not definately

It can sound like an "a" in "def-in-ah-tely," but the word is spelled with an "i."

2. When do we use "then" or "than"?

I see confusion over then/than all the time.

We write "then" when the topic is related to time or a sequence of events. As in, "I am going to the park and then to the store."

"Than" comes into play when we compare or assess. As in, "The comedian is funnier than I expected."

3. Assure, ensure or insure?

The trio are all so similar. When do we use each one?

Assure is to calm someone's nerves or tell them it's OK.

Ensure is to make certain.

Insure is to cover or protect (often in a financial sense).

4. No apostrophes in plural words

I don't know when the apostrophe situation began, but I see the error all the time. Someone will write on Facebook, "So excited for all the concert's this summer!"

Nope. Incorrect. It's "concerts." Always has been.

Instead, we use apostrophes to show possession ("Danny's article has writing tips"). Leaders need to know better.

5. Should you use "their" or "its"?

Here's another common mistake most of us don't think about. For example, "I learned a lot about the company and **their** approach to customer service."

Wrong. "Their" would refer to a plural noun, but the noun in question is "company."

"I learned a lot about the company and **its** approach to customer service."

"Company" is singular. Always refer to your subject and *then* choose **its** or **their**.

6. When do we use "principal" or "principle"?

A "principle" is a rule. A "principal" is a title like a high school principal.

7. And finally, the word misspell.

Many people think it's "mispell" with a single "s."

But if leaders can't spell "misspell" correctly, then our grammar has a long way to go.

SEVEN PUNCTUATION MISTAKES LEADERS NEVER MAKE

Punctuation is so boring, right? Who cares about those pesky commas, periods and exclamation points?

In the business world, they matter. A lot.

Sloppy punctuation can undermine your intelligence and make people question your ability.

Here are seven punctuation mistakes to avoid. Your reputation as a leader (or aspiring leader) depends on it!

1. Run-on sentences

The first punctuation mistake on our list occurs when there's no punctuation at all because the sentence keeps going when the writer should add a period but instead continues on and there's no end to the line and the reader is worn out but there's no period in sight so when does it all end?

Whew. See what I mean?

Rewritten:

The first punctuation mistake on our list occurs when there's no punctuation at all. The sentence keeps going when the writer should add a period. Otherwise, the reader is worn out, but there's no period in sight. When does it all end?

Read your sentence aloud. Does it *feel* like you go on too long? If so, add a period or two to break up different thoughts/ideas.

2. Way too many commas

A sentence with too many commas, makes our writing hard to process, because we include unnatural stops in the flow of a thought, and it's frustrating, for the reader.

Wasn't that last sentence annoying?

There's no easy answer for reducing comma usage. The best course of action is to read your work aloud and look for places where a comma causes an unnecessary pause.

3. Double exclamation points

Double exclamations have no place in a leader's writing. I make no apologies for that rule.

There's a difference between energetic and overkill, and it happens somewhere between ! and !!

If you're on Gchat or talking to a friend through Gmail, go nuts!!!

But when it comes to work, the double exclamation is double trouble. You need people to feel comfortable using your business. If you drop !! everywhere, it could be seen as a red flag.

4. Ugly hyphens

I think there's a clean way to use hyphens and an ugly way.

The unsightly approach?

Something like:

Lesson 1- Introductions

The hyphen right up against the "1" looks sloppy.

In my opinion, there are two ways to improve "Lesson 1- Introductions."

1. "Lesson 1 – Introductions"
2. "Lesson 1: Introductions"

Option #1 is a dash with space on either side.

Option #2 is a colon. Both choices look better than "Lesson 1-" because they're more orderly.

Whenever you need to separate words for emphasis (ex: in a bulleted list or main title), look out for the misplaced hyphen and make the correction.

5. Emojis

You need a strong relationship with a business professional before you include smiley faces, "prayer hands" and whatever else.

For email introductions and other business correspondence, emojis are a no-go.

6. ALL CAPS

Emails in all caps FEEL LIKE THE WRITER IS SCREAMING AT YOU.

Unclick caps lock, start over and write sentences with normal capitalization.

7. Two spaces after a period

Emails and other online content call for one space after a period. Two spaces over and over throughout a blog post or website content will drive readers crazy. I mean, *crazy.*

One space and you're done. Every time.

SEVEN EMAIL MISTAKES LEADERS NEVER MAKE

When we send business emails to open doors or grow our company/organization, every word and punctuation mark matter.

If we use the wrong word or phrase, we can turn the recipient off. That means a single writing gaffe could doom a new opportunity. Seems harsh, but it happens every day. Here are seven to avoid:

1. Don't bury the lead

With most networking emails, we need to include a "big ask."

- Ask for a coffee chat

- Ask for someone to put in a word about a job

- Ask a colleague to connect you to another person

The key with the "big ask" is to not bury it. Otherwise, you sound like a timid rookie. ("Please, won't you help me?")

11

If "the ask" comes near the beginning, you look confident and sure of yourself. ("I know what I'm doing.")

2. Don't use the wrong name or company

Sometimes, we need to send the same general email to several different people, but the emails go out one person at a time.

In those moments, be extra careful about the person's name and, if included, the person's company. Otherwise, it's awkward to send an email to someone but include the name of the person who received your previous email. Yikes.

3. Limit the use of pronouns

"Hey, did you get that done yet?"

"I gave all of them to the client."

"When will he be ready?"

Meanwhile, the reader thinks, "What is that? What are them? Who is he?"

As you write, keep a close watch on the number of pronouns. The words are often vague and make it difficult for people to know what you mean.

Do a quick search for the following words and consider if you should replace with the actual noun.

- this
- that
- these
- those
- he/him
- she/her
- it
- they
- them
- their

- we
- us
- our

4. Always remember the email could be forwarded

Email has a mind all its own.

A single message can travel from one inbox to another with lightning speed, and before you know it, a note to a friend lands on someone's screen across town or around the globe.

Once you press "Send" you lose all control. That's why you should write every business email with the expectation the reader will forward it along.

5. Easy on the acronyms and jargon

Let's say you're a researcher for a pharmaceutical company and work in a division called RDT. You use the expression "RDT" 25 times a day, and to you the acronym obviously means "Research and Development Team."

To anyone outside of your team — possibly at the same company — RDT means... well, nothing.

Every time you include an acronym in an email — or resume, cover letter and presentation — you must follow one basic rule: provide the full name of the acronym on first reference.

6. Never respond to emails "in your head"

We've all been there. In your mind, you 100% responded to that work email. But in reality, the message never went out and people on the other end might anxiously await a reply.

They wonder, "Did she see my email? Did it go to spam? Do I need to send it again?"

A quick "Thanks. I received your email." and all those questions disappear. Keep the emails in the computer, not in your brain.

7. Slow down with the follow ups

Finally, when *you're* the one who needs a response, how soon is too soon to check back in?

If you need an urgent response, it's fine to reach out to the person after 1-2 hours. But if, for example, you requested someone to help you network, give the person at least two days to respond before you come around with a reminder email.

Yes, always advocate for yourself and your business. But also allow people to respond on their own schedule. It's a fine balance, to be sure.

HOW TO BE BRIEF AND POLITE AT THE SAME TIME

In business communication, there's a supreme value on the ability to say a lot in a small space. People are busy and need you to "get to the point."

Too often, though, the pursuit of brevity makes us come across as blunt or short — particularly in email conversations.

I believe the best leaders understand how to be brief and polite at the same time. The point is to be mindful of how people might perceive our words.

Here's an example from someone who is brief but also blunt.

Hi everyone,

Still lots of work to do on Project Alpha.

Gina — you need to check our data again to be certain the numbers add up.

Steve — stop by my office on Tuesday when you can.

Marshall — are you ready with the analysis, or do you need more time?

Thanks,

– Barry

Barry's email is short, no doubt. But his terseness leaves a lot of questions and gray area. Let's break it down.

Still lots of work to do on Project Alpha.

Is Barry happy with the team's progress or not? We can't tell.

Gina — you need to check our data again to be certain the numbers add up.

Which numbers, in particular, should Gina check again?

Steve — stop by my office on Tuesday when you can.

Is Steve in trouble? Is this a friendly chat? Who knows!

Marshall — are you ready with the analysis, or do you need more time?

Does Barry think Marshall is falling behind? Or not? Again, we aren't sure.

Here's a revised email so Barry is brief but also polite. In doing so, he also demonstrates leadership.

Hi everyone,

Thanks for your efforts so far on Project Alpha. We still have a lot of work to do before the project is completed.

Gina — can you please check our data again to be certain the numbers add up? In particular, make sure our efficiency stats are 100% correct.

Steve — stop by my office on Tuesday when you can. I finally have feedback from upstairs about your Project Beta proposal.

Marshall — are you ready with the analysis, or do you need more time? Let me know.

Thanks, everyone.

– Barry

Doesn't email #2 seem like a different person than email #1? The message is brief, but there's a more optimistic tone. Plus, email #2 helps Barry appear as a supportive leader rather than a difficult manager.

Let's break it down line by line.

Thanks for your efforts so far on Project Alpha. We still have a lot of work to do before the project is completed.

Friendly and encouraging. A tone setter for the entire message.

Gina — can you please check our data again to be certain the numbers add up? In particular, make sure our efficiency stats are 100% correct.

Now, Barry is clear on what, exactly, he would like Gina to check on.

Steve — stop by my office on Tuesday when you can. I finally have feedback from upstairs about your Project Beta proposal.

This time, Steve knows what Barry plans to discuss. Not as scary anymore!

Marshall — are you ready with the analysis, or do you need more time? Let me know.

In email #1, it felt as if Barry called out Marshall for not having finished on time. Now, we know it's not that serious.

Before you send an email to your team — or, frankly, to anyone in your business network — ask yourself:

▸ Do I have a lot of short sentences that end in periods?

▸ Does it feel like my responses are hurried or missing detail?

▸ If I were working under me, would this email throw me off?

If any of the answers is "yes," then here are some simple fixes.

▸ Instead of one-word answers, think how you can add a bit of a longer reply. I don't mean write 300 words, but imagine if you were face to face with the email recipient. Would you only use the word "Fine." in your response? What would you actually say?

▸ Before you dive right into a request, command or critique, could you add a bit of conversation? No, don't dance around a sensitive subject. But if the topic is benign enough, make the email feel like a conversation and not a robotic, emotionless exchange.

▸ When in doubt, print out the email and look at the message on paper. Read it aloud. Does your inflection seem off? If so, edit the message so you come across friendlier.

Again, when you're in charge, every word matters so watch your tone. Believe me, your employees will.

NAME-DROPPING FOR LEADERSHIP

What do employees crave from their bosses?

Aside from a raise or promotion, it's recognition for a job well done.

That's why, with email and in-person situations, leaders should "name-drop" employees who have performed at a high level or made strides on a given project/ challenge.

The move simultaneously improves your standing as a leader and earns respect from co-workers and colleagues.

Here's an example for an email situation:

You finished a big presentation to a potential new client. You, the president, brought along two other team members for the pitch, and you want to update the entire team (15 people) on how it went.

The forgettable approach to thank the two team members would be:

And great work by our team on the Acme presentation. I think we impressed the Acme folks in the room.

What an opportunity wasted to thank team members in front of the rest of the company. By writing "our team," it minimizes the role the two people played.

The "name-drop" line could look something like:

And great work by Ashley and Don on the Acme presentation. I think you both impressed the Acme folks in the room with our PowerPoint — it looked sharp.

Now, Ashley and Don feel valued and receive their due recognition. The leader name-drops both of them in a way that's genuine and sincere.

17

What about an in-person conversation? The strategy works the same way but requires even greater awareness of the moment. Unlike an email, the name-drop happens in real time.

Perhaps, at the next all-hands company meeting, you discuss current and future projects. Don't gloss over the team member who went with you to the Acme presentation.

Thanks to the team members who came with me on the Acme pitch.

Instead, remember to "name-drop" and give the two staff members their moment in the sun.

And I want to make a special note to thank Ashley and Don on the Acme presentation. I think you both impressed the Acme folks in the room with our PowerPoint — it looked sharp.

Ashley and Don win the "gold star" for the day and feel like their work is appreciated.

All from a simple name-drop. What could be easier?

AVOID GIANT PARAGRAPHS

To appear confident and in control, leaders should ascribe to the motto "Less is more." If you write too much in a single paragraph, it can overwhelm the reader and, worse yet, appear sloppy. Long-winded sentences and paragraphs make it seem like your thoughts are scrambled and that you don't know how to say a lot in a small amount of space. The writing style wears out your readers and can impact your leadership. It's as if you need to keep going and going because you feel people don't believe you — like a used car salesman who won't stop "selling" because he wants you to buy a "lemon" of a car. And finally, you step back and look at what you created and you realize: it's a giant, bloated paragraph no one wants to read.

Wouldn't it be better if I wiped out that entire paragraph and instead made the message short and sweet? For example:

Remember, when it comes to writing messages to your team, less is more.

Fewer words = more confidence.

Sharper message = more understandable.

That's why a well-crafted email, letter, memo or other piece of professional writing has two phases:

- Rough draft
- Final draft

You may write, for instance, a rough draft of an email and find it contains a large paragraph like the one I wrote at the beginning of this section.

And you know what? That's OK.

Often, the rough draft is our stream of consciousness, and the words flow from our brains right onto the page without a lot of strategy or planning.

But you should never press "Send" on a rough draft. Now is the time to step back and evaluate what you wrote. The first question should be, "Do I have any large paragraphs?" If so, break out the butcher's knife and chop up the sentences.

Your choices are to either turn one big paragraph into several "mini" paragraphs (2–3 sentences max) or to remove the entire paragraph and replace it with the central thought or argument contained in the section.

Ask yourself, "If I only had 10 seconds to make my point, what would I write?"

The answer will be much, much shorter than the big paragraph from the rough draft.

Once you read a final draft, review once more for typos/misspellings and *then* send out the message.

You will feel better about what you wrote AND the readers (ex: your employees) will respect you for conveying a lot in a small space.

ONE COMMA OR TWO IN EMAIL INTROS?

Proper grammar insists we use a comma between a greeting and a person's name.

Example: Hi, Bob

However, with email introductions we also need to put a comma after the person's first name as a way to lead off the message.

Example: Hi, Bob,

I believe the double comma (Hi, Bob,) is awkward and impacts the readability of an email.

Throughout the book, I recommend people use the single comma after the name (Hi Bob,) because it's a cleaner way to greet someone.

Of course, you can choose the comma option you prefer.

But now you know where I stand.

CAPITALIZATION FOR INTEROFFICE COMMS?

What are the rules of communication with your own team?

How should we correspond through tools like Slack that encourage instant-message style conversations rather than a slow-moving email chain?

Internal comms programs are a new-ish tool in the office and for remote workers. That means there aren't hard-and-fast rules around what's most appropriate.

May I be so bold as to create a list of best practices for the thousands of quick messages you, as a leader, send to people on your team.

- ▸ As a leader in your company/organization, you must maintain your status even if the chitchat in the program can seem casual. It's like gathering at a virtual watercooler; you need to be on your best behavior.

- ▸ Start sentences with capital letters and capitalize proper nouns until the co-worker on the other end proves he/she prefers lowercase words at all times. For example: "Do you have the report for the Nicholson account yet?"
  - ○ Once the other person shows a preference for lowercase words, you may choose to go with, "do you have the report for the nicholson account yet?"
  - ○ If you type with the case the other person prefers, you are always in the right.

- ▸ In the same vein, stay away from emojis until the other person drops one first.

- ▸ Even though the chatter through instant messages can be rapid fire, watch every word you type. Many communication tools act as archives so anyone with access can find past conversations in the program.

○ Plus, a two or three-person dialogue can, the next day, include several more people. Maybe one of the new people wasn't supposed to read a message that appeared a day before? Uh oh.

▶ When the message thread includes clients, my opinion is to maintain proper rules of capitalization at all times — even if the other person is into lowercase writing and abbreviations.

○ The client pays you for a service, and you should maintain a high level of professionalism.

Chapter 2
Write to Your Team

Before you write, you must listen

We place so much importance today on tweeting, posting, sharing and commenting that we forget about the most important verb in the workplace.

Listen.

This is not a third-grade lesson in making friends. We *know* we're supposed to listen to each other, but how often do we put away our phones and hear every single word someone has to say?

Probably not often enough.

The best leaders at a company give their employees the floor *and* the time of day. They are patient, don't interject and use feedback to drive the business forward.

Yes, bosses are in charge but that doesn't mean they need to dominate every conversation.

How do you, as a leader (or emerging leader), develop expert listening skills? There are two steps:

1. Develop a "listening mind-set"

2. Practice practice practice

What's a "listening mind-set"?

First and foremost, you don't listen to employees so you can jump in and tell them what's what. You track their every word so you can follow up with thoughtful questions to take the conversation deeper.

The dialogue is a great opportunity to use my "6 Most Powerful Words in Networking." They are:

- ▸ WHO

- ▸ WHAT

- ▸ WHEN

- ▸ WHERE

- ▸ WHY

- ▸ HOW

Rather than jump in and take over the conversation, think about the questions you can ask that relate to what the person said most recently.

Wrong way to listen

Employee: The Richards account has been difficult from the start, and it's obvious our team wasn't on the same page.

Boss: I had a feeling the Richards project would be a problem because we've had issues with other members of the Richards team in the past. This is what you need to do from now on...

The employee was about to explain what went wrong and, perhaps, offer a solution to a client management problem. But the boss pretty much took over the conversation and never *listened*.

Right way to listen

Employee: The Richards account has been difficult from the start, and it's obvious our team wasn't on the same page.

*Boss: **Why** do you think it's been difficult?*

Employee: Well, we struggled to find times for everyone to meet so we had trouble communicating and keeping everyone on the same page.

*Boss: **How** do you think everyone should have stayed in communication?*

Employee: I think it was too much to ask the Richards team to meet twice a month. Maybe once a month and regular conference calls instead?

Boss: I like that idea. Good thinking.

The boss allows the employee to talk further by asking questions (**why** and **how** are two of the "Six Most Powerful Words in Networking").

A leader at a company doesn't need to create brilliant ideas out of thin air. Why not listen intently to the team and let people share insights that can guide the organization?

The only way to gain new perspective is to stop what you're doing and fall into a "listening mind-set."

Say to yourself, "I am going to be the listener and questioner for the next few minutes." Let's see what intel I can uncover.

Leader and Listener. Two words that look and sound awfully similar.

There's a reason for that.

Manage the team

HOW TO ASSIGN ROLES OR RESPONSIBILITIES

The best leaders understand the power of delegation.

For one, you divide up the work. Why put everything on yourself?

Plus, delegation empowers your employees. The approach shows you believe in your team members and makes everyone more capable.

When it's time to delegate, the email template that follows will help you strike the right tone.

Subject line: Assigning tasks for [name of project; for instance, "the Alpha project"]

Hi everyone,

[Set up the discussion; for instance, "As we move ahead with the Alpha project, I need all of us to take on different roles to make sure everything stays on track."]

> *Note: The use of "I" shows you are confident and in charge. The use of "us" underscores how everyone on the team will work hard on the project — including you.*

I know if we all do our part, the project will be a success.

[Then, explain your role and what you need from others; for instance, "I will kick off conversations with the top brass at Alpha; we have an introductory video conference on Tuesday at 11 a.m.

In the meantime, please look for your name and make a note of what you need to do.

- **Damian:** Manage the research component and report back to us on the survey findings by July 12.

- **Jess:** Be the front-facing team member to the Alpha folks. Please schedule an initial meeting for some time next week.

- **Martin:** Review the current Alpha website to understand the company's philosophy and recent history.

- **Dan:** Develop a contact list for all Alpha employees engaged on the project."]

[Finally, share any next steps; for instance, "We can recap all of our efforts at the next staff meeting on July 8."]

If you have questions, give me a call.

Thanks,

– Leader's first name

Email signature

Deeper Insight

Be straightforward but strike a tone that conveys you also have a role on the project. In that way, you delegate but claim responsibility too. You're in the fight with the rest of your team, and the employees will take notice.

Also consider using bold and even yellow highlight on employees' names so the words jump out.

HOW TO TELL A TEAM MEMBER HE/SHE DID A GREAT JOB

As a leader in your company/organization, it's important to dispense praise when appropriate. Why? The move helps you build trust and authority at the same time.

It's easy to say, "Nice job!" or "Great going!" and leave it at that. But the best leaders understand they must take the compliment a step further. They need to provide an explanation on what they appreciate.

The **what** and the **why**: essential details for leaders up and down an organizational chart.

Here's an example: Let's say you noticed your employee go above and beyond for a customer. Whether in person, over the phone or through an email, follow the **what/why** formula.

You: Hi Brian, I want to thank you for how you treated that stubborn client yesterday from Acme Corporation.

Brian: Oh, thanks. It was no big deal. Just doing my job.

You: No, I saw how tough he was about the tri-fold brochure we designed. He made multiple changes *after* we showed him a final proof. But you kept your cool and made sure he was happy in the end. Acme is a big account for us so thank you for the extra effort.

Brian: Absolutely. I knew if I stayed calm we would resolve the problem.

You: Yep, exactly.

————

Did you see the **what** and the **why?**

What: …multiple changes *after* we showed him a final proof.

Why: Acme is a big account for us so thank you for the extra effort.

As in all writing scenarios, the details make the difference. A fuller explanation (what/why) gives the compliment greater significance and strengthens your position as a leader — especially with the employee you praised.

It's not enough to tell someone, "Well done!" Provide the *reason* for the praise, and your leadership skills will grow before your eyes.

HOW TO WRITE THE "LONG-TERM VISION" EMAIL

When you write a "big idea" or long-term planning email, the danger is to include too much.

If your employees open an email and are smacked right away with 14 giant paragraphs that scroll and scroll, they will recoil and dread the 30 minutes they need to spend sifting through your manifesto.

That's why, when a leader sends a "big idea" email to assess the road ahead, the message needs to accomplish two ends:

▸ Lay out a vision or plan in as few words as possible

▸ Set up further in-person (or virtual) discussion

The email should not become the start of a chain with 137 messages from 12 different people. The message also shouldn't prompt a planning session through an internal communication tool or instant message. Both approaches are inefficient (and annoying).

Your email needs to set the tone and agenda so when everyone meets face to face, they have a starting point for dialogue.

That's why I suggest a long-term planning email like the one below.

Subject line: Looking ahead to [the milestone or benchmark; for instance, "the new year"]

Hi everyone,

[First, set up the discussion; for instance, "As we think about the new year and our business goals, I have laid out some big ideas on the direction I feel we need to go. We will reconvene after January 1 to discuss these points and hopefully refine them further as a group."]

> NOTE: Right away, you explain the email is a starting point and that you plan to expand further during a group discussion.

[Then, lay out your ideas in a bulleted or numbered list. For instance:

1. "We've seen tremendous growth in our medical sales vertical in Q4. I want to brainstorm new ways we can tap into that space and generate new leads."
2. Strategy or big idea #2 that's a similar length to #1
3. Strategy or big idea #3 that's a similar length to #1
4. Strategy or big idea #4 that's a similar length to #1]

> NOTE: You can go past four ideas, but if the list becomes too long, then it's difficult for people to retain all the information. Less is more.

Please do some thinking on your own and be prepared to talk through these action items [during a future conversation; for instance, "at our staff meeting. Of course, I welcome your own thoughts on how to attack the new year."]

I look forward to the discussion,

– Leader's first name

Email signature

Deeper Insight

Again, the email is plainly written and designed to kickstart face-to-face conversation rather than 10,000 words everyone feels compelled to slog through.

Set the table, lay out next steps and then talk it out.

HOW TO EXPLAIN A COMPLEX TOPIC IN SIMPLE TERMS

Often leaders need to explain intricate or weighty subjects in a clear, understandable way. In those moments, strong writing skills are paramount.

You don't want to confuse people when you try to break down a difficult topic. On the flip side, employees will appreciate how you simplified the issue and, in doing so, valued their time and attention.

Here's an example:

Subject line: [The explanation; for instance, "Why we decided to change health care providers"]

Hi everyone,

[Speak to the pressing issue right away; for instance, "I know there are rumblings in the office about why we chose to switch health care providers."]

[Then, explain the complex topic piece by piece; for instance, "The decision had a lot of moving parts so I will explain everything the simplest way I can.

Our previous health care plan had become too costly so we initially hired a consultant, Brad Sherwood, to evaluate next steps.

We then learned Brad was financially invested in one health care option, Acme Health, and could not rely on him for an objective assessment.

We almost chose to stay in our current situation but at the last minute learned of a new provider, Acme Choice Plus, which offers stronger coverage for maternity care than what we had.

Through employee feedback, we know maternity care is priority #1.

After weighing the numbers, we opted for Acme Choice Plus. With health care, there is no perfect option, but we believe we have made the most prudent decision for our employees and their families."]

[Finally, wrap up the message; for instance, "Thanks for your understanding. If you have specific questions about the health care plan, please reach out to Ron Sanchez, head of HR, at 555-555-5555 or Ron@email.com."]

– Leader's first name

Email signature

Deeper Insight

Notice the two tactics that make the complex issue understandable.

1. **Short sentences:** There are no blocky paragraphs so it's easier to follow the email all the way to the end.

2. **One foot in front of the other:** The leader explains what took place step by step without wandering off on a tangent or losing focus. Rather, the leader tells the team what happened in an untangled way.

HOW TO CREATE AN EMPLOYER/MENTOR RELATIONSHIP

As a leader, it's important to keep a watchful eye on employees and look for opportunities for professional growth.

If you see how one employee's knowledge base can help someone else, then send an email to connect the two people.

Certainly, you should brief the employee about the mentor opportunity *before* the email goes out. No surprises.

Subject line: Learning from [first and last name of employee; for instance; "Jack Martin"]

Hi [first name of junior employee],

I know you're working hard to learn [the task at hand; for instance, "our elaborate sales process"], and I think it would be helpful to take some pointers from [name of mentor; for instance, "Jack Martin, one of our most senior sales reps"].

I have copied [first name of mentor] on this email. Please find time this week to meet face to face and chat.

Thanks to you both,

– Leader's first name

Email signature

Deeper Insight

Notice the opening line: "I know you're working hard…"

This email is not an opportunity to come down on employees but rather raise them up. Leaders should use their words to motivate.

Also see the final line: "Please find time this week…"

The leader did not write, "I hope you can find time" or "When you have time…"

No, the meet-up is a directive and not a suggestion. There's a level of authority in that line and both people will feel it.

HOW TO PASS ALONG SMART ADVICE OR USEFUL TIPS

Leaders should always try to empower employees with sage advice. The key is to teach in moderation.

If you send out messages three times a week with quotes and leadership parables, the move will become stale.

If you pass along valuable advice once or maybe twice a month, the approach will enhance your value.

And whenever possible, it's best to put the advice in the form of an anecdote. People never forget a great story.

Subject line: [Advice you wish to share; for instance, "Lessons learned at the Acme Global Summit"]

Hi everyone,

[First, set up the message; for instance, "At the Acme Global Summit this past week, I watched a fantastic speaker lead a sales presentation, and I want you to know why she was so effective."]

[Then, share the advice; for instance, "As you read the bulleted list below, think about how you can incorporate her techniques into your own sales pitches.

- The woman, Julie Kim, showcased her tool called Acme CRM (that stands for customer relationship management). Before she ever discussed the product's specs, she led off with a fabulous story.

  o The CRM, through a series of twists and turns, helped connect Julie with an associate producer at Acme Film Studio in Hollywood. The associate producer passed her to an executive producer and eventually the CEO. Today, Acme Film Studio is among the company's clients.

- o **The lesson: Lead the presentation with a story to grab the audience and impart our value.**

- Julie made the presentation hands on. She had everyone use their phones to see how difficult it is to capture leads without a comprehensive CRM tool.

- o **The lesson: Keep people in the crowd engaged so they don't become bored.**

- Finally, I liked her approach at the end to encourage people to schedule demos. We push for demos too, but she had three tablets at her exhibit booth. As she wrapped up, people used the tablets to book appointments.

- o **The lesson: Let's reevaluate our "closing" process at the end of presentations and see how we can line up more appointments."**]

[Lastly, provide a next step; for instance, "At the start of our next staff meeting, we will take five minutes and chat about this email a bit more. We can always improve our sales pitch even in small ways."]

Thanks,

– Leader's first name

Email signature

Deeper Insight

It's not easy to share advice over email that none of the email recipients experienced firsthand. That's why it's important to keep the sentences brief, use bullet points and include a separate line called "The lesson" so employees don't miss the good stuff.

You should encourage all employees to be the "eyes and ears" of the company if they spot a smart tactic out in the field. Sharing fresh techniques will only make your team better and more capable.

HOW TO SETTLE A TEAM DISPUTE OR CONFLICT

Email is a rough place to sort out a conflict — no matter the situation.

An email chain doesn't allow for productive dialogue. Worse yet, employees can read a sentence the wrong way and become offended or turned off.

That's why, to settle a dispute, leaders should plan a face-to-face conversation. And a leader should take pains to ensure the discussion does not unfold in peoples' inboxes.

Subject line: Meeting to discuss [issue at hand; "our new office layout"]

Hi [first names of people involved; for instance, "Samantha, Jon and Reed,"]

[Discuss the issue at hand; for instance, "I know there's been a lot of chatter about our new office layout and where your desks will be located."]

[Then, share a solution or the initial steps to reach one; for instance, "Rather than hold the conversation over email, I want us to meet in person and find compromise on the office layout. I'm confident we can do so as a group."]

[Finally, you may want to share a concrete action item; for instance, "Let's gather in the conference room at 2 p.m. today."]

Thanks,

– Leader's first name

Email signature

Deeper Insight

DO NOT try to hold a dialogue among multiple parties over email. It's an ineffective way to solve problems and won't reflect well on your leadership style.

Put the necessary parties in a room together and make everyone agree to a plan that's fair. Bottom line: don't let problems fester. Deal with them as they arise and move on.

HOW TO CRAFT EMPLOYEE MOTIVATIONAL EMAILS

If you like to send motivational emails to your team, you must have a strategic plan for every piece of content you include.

Do employees feel compelled to read the email because their boss sent it? Yes. Can the email still be packed with knowledge and value every time? Absolutely. The best employee motivational emails contain two main concepts:

- Inspiration
- Practical instruction

That way, when employees close the email they feel empowered and also receive actionable advice they can apply on the job.

Inspiration ideas:

- Quotes on leadership, motivation, hustle, etc.

- An example of how employees demonstrated leadership, motivation, etc.

  - Be sure to explain **exactly** how the person/people stood out. It's not enough to say, "Big thanks to John and Stacy on the Acme proposal." Share the action items John and Stacy took to finish out the proposal.

- Your own observations about leadership, motivation, etc. that you want to pass along.

Practical instruction ideas:

- Links to "life hack" articles and motivational content that will help your employees on the job.

- Information on company policies or other tips and tricks for navigating the organization.

- Tips for goal setting, project management, client relations or other topics relevant to the work you do.

Above all, be mindful of the reader's time. Give a little inspiration and a little practical advice. Then wrap it up.

Less is more with motivational emails. But if your content is useful every time, your team will enjoy the messages and view you as a genuine leader.

HOW TO PREP YOUR TEAM FOR A MEETING

The best leaders want people on their team to shine at all times. That's why it's smart to prep your people before a meeting or event, either internal or external (ex: with a client).

Use the template below to make sure your directions come across.

Subject line: Preparing for the [name of meeting; for instance, "Acme client engagement meeting"]

Hi [first names of team members; for instance, "Pat and Stephanie,"]

[Explain why you need to provide information prior to the meeting; for instance, "Before we meet with the Acme team for the first time this year, it's important you both have background information on the company. I also want you to prepare to talk about different aspects of the project."]

[Provide information here that all team members should know; for instance, "First, make a note that Acme has a new vice president of sales. Scott

Webster left the company in March, and the new vice president is Lynette Odom. She has a lot of experience in sales but doesn't know all the Acme lingo yet."]

[Then give directions to each person. For instance:

"**Pat:** Bring your spreadsheets from Q2 and be ready to discuss the trends you saw in Acme's social media growth.

Stephanie: When Lynette inevitably asks about our new billing structure, I want you to jump in and explain."]

[Finally, give an action item; for instance, "Let's all meet outside Acme's offices 20 minutes before the meeting so we can prepare one more time."]

Thanks, and let me know if you have questions.

– Leader's first name

Email signature

Deeper Insight

First, provide background information the entire group should know. Then, call out employees by name (consider bold and yellow highlight so the person can spot his/her name) and give specific instruction.

Success in a client meeting is all about the preparation *before* the meeting takes place. The email above will keep you, as team leader, on track.

Provide various updates

HOW TO SUMMARIZE THE STATUS OF A PROJECT

As a team leader, it's critical to remain in control as projects evolve. Your team members will instinctively look to you for direction and the roles they need to play.

The email template below will help you shape the message the right way.

Subject line: Updates on [project name; for instance, "Project Beta"]

Hi everyone,

[Set up the message; for instance, "As Project Beta moves along, it's important we have the latest info and understand our roles in the coming weeks. **Please read this email carefully and note where your name appears.**"]

[If there's a special update you need to include first, do so here; for instance, "First, make a note that we will NOT use the original Project Beta logo. You should proceed with the logo called 'NewCursiveLogo' for all marketing materials."]

> NOTE: Then, list out each update or action item as a bullet point. Let people absorb every piece of information one at a time so nothing is lost in a big paragraph. Also, add a space between each bullet so they're not crammed together. Again, let the words breathe.

> Whenever possible, call people out by name and put the name in yellow highlight. That way, the person will see what he/she needs to do.

[For example:

- **"Cindy,** I need you to solicit feedback from at least five current clients on our prototype.

- **James,** before the week is out we need printing cost estimates from at least three printers.

- **Lee,** see if you can find the old photos of our founders working on Project Alpha back in the 1980s. Those pictures would be a nice touch on our website."]

Thanks, and let's keep pushing to get the project done.

– Leader's first name

Email signature

Deeper Insight

The email is decisive but not dictatorial. And there's a huge difference in tone. The sentence at the top commands attention: "Please read this email carefully and note where your name appears."

Also the word "please" appears in the above sentence but never again in the email. If the leader writes "please" for every request, the word becomes stale, and the tone suggests the person is afraid to give direction. One "please" near the beginning is enough.

HOW TO RECAP A TEAM MEETING

After a phone call or meeting, what's the best way for a leader to recap what was covered and dole out responsibilities?

The keys are to keep the message short and ensure everyone knows what they need to do next.

Subject line: Recap of [conference call/meeting/phone call] on [month and day]

Hi everyone,

We had a solid meeting today about the [task/project; for instance, "Acme theme park construction"]. Let's keep everything rolling so the project stays on track.

[If there's a big issue or main point, put it here; for instance, "The top concern right now is the data set about projected crowd sizes on the various rides.

Again, Alicia from Acme expects us to show her the data by Friday, June 8 so let's make that agenda item priority #1."]

NOTE: Don't write "by Friday" because it's too vague. Include the calendar date so there's no way someone on your team would say, "Oh, I thought you meant NEXT Friday." Obviously, miscommunication on the due date can throw off your progress in a significant way.

These are the action items [over the next few days/over the next week/ moving forward]:

NOTE: Then, list out each update or action item as a bullet point. Let people absorb every piece of information one at a time so nothing is lost in a big paragraph. Also, add a space between the bullets so each line has room to breathe.

Whenever possible, call people out by name and put the name in yellow highlight. That way, the person will see what he/she needs to do.

[For instance:

- **"Brandon,** we need your renderings for the Crazy-8 Roller Coaster by 5 p.m. today (Tuesday).

- **Tia** will check with the Acme sales team about any new sponsors we need to incorporate into the rides.

- **Kevin** and **Gabe** (lucky dogs) will go to Super Fun Park USA on Thursday, June 7 to observe the infrastructure and how the crowds move throughout the park. Don't have too much fun without us."]

NOTE: If it's in your personality and feels natural to do so, toss in a little humor now and then.

- **Rafael,** reply all to this email and show everyone video of the Tokyo roller coaster you mentioned in our meeting."]

Thanks, and let me know if there are any questions. [Any additional info; for instance, "I'll be at my desk today until 5:30 p.m."]

– Leader's first name

Email signature

___

Deeper Insight

The best leaders are on top of the latest action items. An email within a couple hours of the meeting will allow you to come across that way.

HOW TO GIVE AN ORGANIZATIONAL UPDATE

Sometimes, emails are no fun to write *or* to read.

When the messages are full of bland instructions or corporate goings-on, it can be a challenge to keep the reader's attention all the way to the end.

How can we turn an otherwise boring email into one that's engaging and maybe — just maybe — a little fun to read?

The following template will help.

___

Subject line: [Topic at hand; for instance, "New protocols for building exit and entry"]

Hi everyone,

[Explain the nature of the message; for instance, "I need to pass along new rules from HR on how to enter and exit the building from Washington Street and Claiborne Avenue."]

[Underscore that everyone needs to read the information; for instance, "This isn't the most scintillating information, but please read all the way through because it's important for how we access the building every day."]

> NOTE: Consider if you should make light of the tedious, administrative message. It will catch the reader's attention and then encourage the person to keep going. Like a subtle call to action.

42

[Provide any additional information; for instance, "If you're on the internal ops or finance teams, you should use the Claiborne entrance because that side can scan your badges. All other employees need to use the Washington Avenue entrance.

The change goes into effect one week from today — Monday, May 14."]

If you have questions, let me know.

Thanks,

– Leader's first name

Email signature

Deeper Insight

Effective business communication is all about managing expectations. Employees see the subject line about building exit and entry and think, "Ugh, this is gonna be a snoozer of an email."

Anticipating the reaction, you include lines with a bit of personality to keep the message light and fresh (ex: "This isn't the most scintillating information").

You know your own personality so use language that's most comfortable. But the trick is to recognize the information isn't all that fascinating and deliver it in a way people wouldn't expect.

Even through a procedural email, there's still a chance to be memorable.

HOW TO EXPLAIN ORGANIZATIONAL ANNOUNCEMENTS

As a leader, you need to share important information so employees can process each item.

If your "organizational" emails tend to cover the same topics, then you should create a formula to follow each time.

Here's a template example:

Subject line: [Tease the highlights; for instance, "Team updates — Welcome Jon Gibbons, software renewal and more"]

NOTE: Tease a couple of organizational items in the subject line. The tactic will keep your emails unique and entice team members to open them right away. It's a much better approach than the same subject line every time (ex: "Organizational updates").

Hi team,

Good morning/afternoon.

I have several announcements to pass along [this week/this month] so let's get right to it.

[Then, share information as separate items with headlines for better organization. Consider a quote or other motivational tool at the end. Here's a mock email:

Staff Updates

Please welcome Jon Gibbons to our team at Acme Corporation! Jon is a new program analyst and will work mostly on the Jennings account. He's a recent graduate from Big State University and a big fan of all Philly sports. Make sure you say hello to Jon when you see him.

Note: Toss in a little "fun fact" (ex: big fan of all Philly sports) so it's not all about work.

Software Upgrades

By the end of the week, everyone needs to upgrade their version of Graphic Design Pro 3000. Here's the link for the upgrade. Let me know if you run into any issues.

Need One More for Vegas!

Once again, we plan to attend the Big Trade Conference in Las Vegas and have a booth in the main exhibit hall. Stefanie Rios can't make it in the end so we need one person. Who's in? Reply to me ASAP.

Hungry?

There are jelly donuts in the break room courtesy of Acme Copiers and Paper Supply. Get 'em while you can.

Quote of the Week

"Good things happen to those who hustle" — Chuck Noll

Thanks, team.

- Leader's first name

Email signature

Deeper Insight

Stay within your personality but make the email enjoyable for your audience. The best way is to incorporate proper nouns (ex: Philly sports, Graphic Design Pro 3000 and jelly donuts).

Specific language holds the reader's attention and makes you more assertive.

HOW TO DISCUSS RESEARCH, DATA AND OTHER INSIGHTS

Alert! We have entered the email danger zone.

If you have a large amount of data to share with your team, you run the risk of composing an email that's disorganized, too wordy and difficult to follow.

Pass along new research and then provide a few highlights and then link people to deeper information. And then, treat the email as a jump-off point rather than a venue to hold the entire conversation.

Here's the play:

Subject line: [Topic at hand; for instance, "Q1 data about our social media marketing efforts"]

Hi team,

[Set up the message; for instance, "As we move into Q2, it's important to evaluate the numbers from Q1 to see where we can make adjustments. Thanks to Clara for pulling the data together."]

[Put critical information near the top of the message so people see it; for instance, "Please mark your calendars for Thursday, August 9 at 2 p.m. ET for a conference call about the data. We will discuss as a team what needs to change and what we're doing well."]

NOTE: Include time zones (ex: ET) in case you communicate with people in different parts of the country or world. Never assume people know what time zone you reference when you put a time in an email.

[Include any additional information you don't want people to overlook; for instance, "I sent you a calendar invite in a separate email. If you have an issue with the day/time of the conference call, let me know today."]

[Then, share research and data; for instance, "Prior to the call, read the highlights below and click this link to see the full report.

- Data point 1

- Data point 2

- Data point 3

- Data point 4

- Data point 5"]

Thanks,

- Leader's first name

Email signature

Deeper Insight

There are a few subtleties to the template above.

▶ The leader thanks an employee (Clara) for compiling the data. As we discussed on page 6, it's about "we" instead of "I" or "me."

▶ The leader also sets up a conference call and puts the information high up in the email so the recipients will see it. Always put the call to action near the top of your message.

▶ The leader limits the number of data points to five. Any more and the list becomes unruly and hard to follow.

▶ The line reads, "If you have an issue with the day/time of the conference call, let me know today." The word "today" is important. Don't "let me know when you have a chance." No, tell me right now so we can put the meeting on the calendar and have the conversation.

HOW TO SHARE GOOD NEWS

It seems obvious how to share good news. Tell people the positive info and throw in a few exclamation marks, right?

Even a happy report requires attention to detail and a bit of nuance so leaders look their best.

Subject line: Great news about [topic at hand; for instance, "the Peterson RFP"]

Hi everyone,

[Share the news right away; for instance, "I'm excited to report the Peterson Companies selected us to become its new IT partner!"]

> *Note: First, the line above is active voice ("Peterson Companies selected us"). Active voice has an assertive tone. It's better than, "I'm excited to report we have been selected by Peterson Companies to become its new IT partner." Do you feel the difference?*

> *Second, I believe exclamation marks in business emails are reserved for special occasions. And the Peterson Companies announcement qualifies. It's a big deal!*

[Share credit where credit is due; for instance, "Thank you to everyone who worked so hard on the RFP. It was no picnic to revise the capabilities section three times (shout out to Ricardo on all the updates), but I believe the extra effort made the difference."]

> *Note: Give a specific detail about the positive news or a reason why the positive news came about (ex: Ricardo's extra effort). Take the email deeper than a simple, "We did it!"*

[Finally, explain what happens now; for instance, "As for next steps, keep an eye on your email over the next two weeks. I will have a date/time soon from the Peterson team for a kickoff meeting."]

Thanks, everyone.

– Leader's first name

Email signature

Deeper Insight

To recap the template:

▸ Use active voice to announce the news and put the main information at the top.

▸ Give at least one specific detail about your team's efforts that led to the big win. Make sure you don't focus on one person and then forget to note the accomplishments of others. If you need to call out each person, do it.

▸ Provide info on any next steps so your team knows what's to come.

HOW TO SHARE BAD NEWS

It's no fun to share bad news, but that task usually falls to the leader.

When it's time to address your team, be up front and show how the company plans to address the problem or make changes.

Scenario 1: Company unable to issue bonuses after a slow Q3

Subject line: [Explain the nature of the message; for instance, "Update on bonuses for Q4 2018"]

Hi team,

[Share the bad news right away; for instance, "I want to give you an update on bonuses for Q4 2018. We did not meet our planned billing for the quarter and for that reason are unable to issue bonuses."]

[Give an explanation for the bad news as best you can; for instance, "I know the news is disappointing because we all had high expectations for the last quarter. I believe our total billable hours were down because of vacation time and increased bench time waiting on client staffing and projects to start."]

[Provide a next step to rebound from the bad news; for instance, "That being said, we're off to a strong start this year. Our sales staff has added five new clients since February. We have also found new projects for existing staff who rolled off client engagements in the middle of Q4 last year."]

[Include a wrap-up message to point the team in right direction; for instance, "I am confident in a strong 2019 Q1. And I believe we will again hit our targets and find our stride."]

If anyone has questions, please reach out to me directly.

Thanks for all your hard work,

– Leader's first name

Email signature

Deeper Insight

The biggest takeaway from the email above? The leader shares the "bad news" in the email's opening line.

It's weak, ineffective leadership to hide the main point at the bottom of the email. Come out and explain the situation right away. In short: own it.

The leader also explains *why* there are no bonuses. Again, it would be incomplete to tell employees, "Sorry, no bonuses," but then not explain why. People can accept bad news, but what often drives them crazy is no explanation or context around the decision.

Lastly, the leader allows people to "reach out to me directly." The open-door policy builds trust with employees and maintains strong lines of communication.

Scenario 2: Client not happy with the company's latest efforts

Let's say you're not a manager but rather an entry-level employee or someone who doesn't oversee a team. As an example, maybe you had a rough time with a difficult client and need to relay the experience.

This is how you tell everyone what occurred but avoid looking like a complainer.

Subject line: [Explain the "bad news" right away; for instance, "Lee Forman from Acme not happy with latest renderings"]

Hey everyone,

[Cut to the chase; for instance, "I have a quick update on my meeting with Lee Forman. In short, he was not happy with the latest renderings of the public park. He also told me if we can't deliver a better design by the end of the week he'll need to choose another design partner.

I assured Lee we will jump on it and show him a new rendering ASAP. "]

[Then, explain the next steps; for instance, "Carrie and Deon, can we meet at 3:30 p.m. today and talk about it?"]

Thanks,

– Employee's first name

Email signature

Deeper Insight

First, the subject line shares the bad news right away. No need to tip-toe around the situation; come out and say what's going on.

The intro paragraph of the email also expands on the bad news. The email wastes no time with pleasantries or warming people up before laying out the raw truth.

Still, the writer follows up with next steps ("we will jump on it") and then even schedules a team discussion.

No time to mope. The work must be done.

That's why, no matter where you stand in an organization, it might fall to you to deliver bad news. How you share the information speaks to your character and ability to push through challenging moments.

HOW TO OFFER A WEEKLY "NEWS AND NOTES" MESSAGE

Leaders often need to be the arbiters of information for their teams.

That means you might send "news and notes" emails that summarize the latest company happenings and set the table for the week ahead.

Here's the best way to craft the message.

Subject line: [Provide two to three examples of topics from inside the message; for instance, "Acme updates, welcome Sandy Kim and kitchen renovations"]

> *Note: Why be so specific in the subject line? Because employees will become bored if every single "news and notes" email from you has the same standard subject line (ex: Weekly Team News and Notes). Who would be interested in a generic subject line like that?*

Hi everyone,

[Set up the message and then provide critical updates; for instance, "First off, I want everyone to know about the updates we've made to the Acme project. Many thanks to Joey and Sara for their hard work. Here's the latest:

- The launch date is now set for March 17.

- The client did finally approve the home page rebrand so we can put that issue to rest.

- Acme expects to have a celebrity endorse the new launch, but they won't tell us yet who it is. Secrets, secrets."]

[Then, share additional information the team would find relevant; for instance, "In other news, please welcome our summer intern, Sandy Kim. She's a junior communications major at Big State University and ready to help with various design and marketing projects. Be sure to include Sandy in staff meetings and give her things to do!"]

[Then, include any last pieces of news; for instance, "Finally, all the crazy construction is over in the staff kitchen. We now have granite countertops and a new fridge. It's like a new space."]

[Then, you may consider a quote or other form of motivation; for instance, "As always, I leave you with a motivational quote:

> *"The only person you are destined to become is the person you decide to be." — Ralph Waldo Emerson"]*

Make it a great week,

– Leader's first name

Email signature

Deeper Insight

Consider the same structure for each "news and notes" email. Employees will become familiar with the format and where to find certain pieces of information.

Maintain accountability

THE BALANCE BETWEEN MICROMANAGEMENT AND BEING HANDS OFF

When you assign a task to an employee, what's your next move?

Do you stand over the person's shoulder and make sure he or she does the work?

Or do you walk away and assume the person will complete the job?

Many managers would say the proper recipe is a little bit of both. Give people their space to operate but stay engaged to hold them accountable.

That said, there is a sliding scale. Newer employees often require more oversight than long-time staffers who have shown they can follow through on a task.

In any case, it's impossible to offer hard-and-fast rules on how often to do status checks with employees. Some tasks can be done in an hour and others take months.

Sometimes, leadership is a gut feeling. Ask your inner self:

▸ Has it been too long since your employee gave you an update?

▸ Can you sense the client is anxious?

▸ Has the project started to drag?

If so, consider one of the email templates on the following pages keep employees in check.

HOW TO MAKE SURE EMPLOYEES FOLLOW THROUGH ON TASKS

Subject line: Checking back in on [task at hand; for instance, "the logo redesign for Acme Corporation"]

Hi [employee's first name],

Please give me the status on the [task at hand; "logo redesign for Acme Corporation"].

[Then remind the person why you're checking in; for instance, "Margo, the senior VP at Acme, asked to see the latest mock-ups by today at 4 p.m. Send the designs to me first so I can review."]

Thanks,

– Leader's first name

Email signature

Deeper Insight

The template above is unemotional and procedural. Politely, the leader asks when the employee will finish the logo design.

Now, what if the particular employee *always* finishes work at the deadline (or later) and makes everyone sweat it out? That's when the leader needs to have a sit-down conversation with the employee about planning ahead and better project management.

But the check-in email should not have a mean-spirited or condescending tone. Those words are trapped in cyberspace forever.

Keep the messages professional and talk face to face about accountability if necessary.

HOW TO ENSURE WORK DOESN'T FALL THROUGH THE CRACKS

Few projects wrap up in an afternoon. Many take days, weeks, months or even years to complete.

As a leader (and perhaps project manager), you must place important tasks front and center.

Whether you send an email to one person or a team, organize the message so every action item has time in the spotlight.

Here's how:

Subject line: Keeping up with tasks for [name of project; for instance, "the Smith account"]

Hi [person's first name] or [everyone],

[Set up the reason for your message; for instance, "I know we have a lot going on right now with the Smith account."]

Note: Whether the email is to one person or a group, consider bullet points to keep each task separate and easy to spot.

[Example of bulleted list:

"Please read the list below and look for your name. Then, reply back today with an answer and a status update.

If it's easier to discuss your efforts by phone, give me a call at 555-555-5555.

- **Tina,** what's the expected finish date on the phase two research?

- **Reese,** did you remember to tell Dave Smith we have the prototype ready to show him?

- **Randall,** were you able to provide a tutorial about the project to Dave's two new hires?"]

Thanks,

– Leader's first name

Email signature

Deeper Insight

First, let's examine the structure of the email. Note how the leader's directions appear *before* the bulleted list.

"Please read the list below and look for your name. Then, reply back today with an answer and a status update.

If it's easier to explain by phone, give me a call at 555-555-5555."

Why *before* the list? Why not put instructions at the end of the email?

It's a tactic known as "bottom line up front." Put the most important part of the message high up so the reader won't miss it.

If the leader asked employees at the end to reply back via email or phone, people might not read that far and miss the instruction.

Now, employees read the instructions and *then* find their names in the list. It's a logical one-two combination that makes sense as our eyes move down the screen.

Finally, note how the names are in bold (I prefer yellow highlight too). It's one more way for people to see a part of the message intended for them.

Clear, concise and organized — it's the perfect formula to keep important tasks from falling through the cracks.

HOW TO SEEK FEEDBACK BEFORE A MAJOR DECISION OR NEW IDEA

Leaders know decisions don't happen in a vacuum. They always need to rely on feedback from others before they choose a road to go down.

Consider if you should seek the collective wisdom of your team the next time you have to make a "big call."

The template here is a framework for the conversation.

Scenario: Weighing the decision to enter a new business vertical

---

Subject line: [Explain the decision at hand; for instance, "Team meeting invitation to discuss new business vertical"]

Hi team,

[Lay out the decision; for instance, "Based on strong — and unexpected — sales of our Acme chocolate bars from local hardware stores, we now plan to roll out a strategy to target similar stores in other markets for 2019."]

[Then, explain what you want; for instance, "Before we go too far down the road, I welcome everyone's feedback on the best ways to tackle the new opportunity."]

[Finally, provide supporting details; for instance, "The managers will have a team meeting on hardware stores on **Monday, April 2 at 2 p.m. in the conference room.** Please join us if you can."]

Thanks,

– Leader's first name

Email signature

Deeper Insight

The biggest takeaway? The leader does not ask for feedback over email. Inevitably, the responses will become a big, ugly chain that's impossible to sift through and then draw any firm conclusions.

Instead, the leader invites employees to a conversation on the topic to foster healthy discussion.

And on a deeper level, the invitation implies, "I respect the viewpoints of every member of my team and want each of us to feel some degree of ownership about the direction of our company."

Empower employees so they feel part of the process. *That's* true leadership.

HOW TO CRITIQUE YOUR EMPLOYEE'S WORK

Constructive criticism is essential for team dynamics. If your employees don't improve a little each day, then the company as a whole will languish.

Still, there's a proper way to dispense critiques while you manage the relationship and remain in control as a leader.

I call the approach "considerate strength."

Subject line: Feedback on [topic at hand; for instance, "the draft of your Acme presentation"]

Hi John,

Thanks for sending along the [topic at hand; for instance, "initial draft of the Acme presentation."]

[First, start with what you appreciate about the person's work and be specific; for instance, "Nice job describing the app development we did for Tech Corporation. I like how you stressed Simon's role as the go-between with the client when we were in the time crunch."]

[Then, share how the person can improve; for instance, "I also have a few critiques about the presentation so we are even stronger the next time we pitch to potential clients.

Please make the changes as soon as you can and send back over to me.

- The opening three slides look flat. Not enough color or images. See what you can do to spice things up.

- At 37 slides, the deck is too long for a 20-minute pitch. Can we bring the slide count under 25? Try to combine slides or determine what we can do without. One idea: I think slides 12–14 with additional client testimonials are overkill.

- I see a few misspellings. Use spell check and clean up the copy."]

[Finally, wrap up the message; for instance, "I look forward to the next version. If you have questions, let me know or stop by my office to chat."]

Thanks,

– Leader's first name

Email signature

Deeper Insight

Begin with the positives and then dive into what needs work. Notice how the critiques are unfiltered ("The opening three slides look boring").

I don't mean you should lace into people when they need to fix their work. But don't dance around the issues either.

The balance is what I mean by "considerate strength." Respect your team but push back when the work needs to improve. That's the proper role of a leader.

Communicate with boards

HOW TO DISCUSS NEWS ABOUT DONORS OR SPONSORS

Money.

Whenever the topic arises, a leader must be careful with word choice. Whether cash flow is good or bad, everyone has an opinion on what to do next.

If you need to update your team on news about your donors, investors or sponsors, use the email to provide updates. Save the discussion around $$$ for a meeting — don't attempt to discuss dollars and cents in an email thread.

Subject line: Update on [the topic at hand; for instance, "sponsors for Fall Festival"]

Hi team,

Good morning/afternoon.

[Jump right into the news; for instance, "As the Fall Festival approaches, we have several updates on committed and potential sponsors. I also note below where each of you can step in based on your relationships with sponsors. Please find your name in highlight."]

NOTE: If it makes sense in the context of your message, tell people up front to find their names and the associated action items.

[Then, list off the updates with short bullet points. For instance:

- "Acme Corporation is committed as our $10,000 title sponsor! **Dana,** please ask Jim Gaskins at Acme for a hi-res company logo and brief description (jim@acme.com).

- We have asked Tech Corporation and ABC Corporation to be Silver sponsors ($5,000) but have not heard back. **Raj,** can you check on both?

- **Lloyd,** what's the status on the sponsor board we will place near the registration table?"]

NOTE: It's a subtle move, but notice how the leader uses "please" one time for Dana's note but not in the other two bullets. The first "please" covers all the other requests because using "please" over and over is redundant and a bit awkward.

Let me know if anyone has questions at this point.

Thanks,

– Leader's first name

Email signature

Deeper Insight

Everyone will appreciate an email that's succinct and provides clear action items when necessary.

Don't be afraid to call people out by name with a yellow highlight. You're not forceful or overbearing. Rather, you make sure people don't overlook their responsibilities.

Try to avoid an email with way too much text or explanation. Push yourself to boil down the message to the essentials. If there is too much information for an email, consider a message that sets up a phone or in-person discussion. For instance:

Hi everyone,

We have a lot of updates related to Fall Festival sponsorships. It's easier to discuss everything as a group than over email.

Let's meet in my office at 4 p.m. today to discuss.

Thanks,

– Leader's first name

Email signature

What's the most efficient path from point A to point B? When you need to convey important information, that's the question every time.

HOW TO SHARE CHANGES THAT CAME OUT OF A BOARD MEETING

If your company/organization has a board, then you may need to relay board meeting information back to employees or other stakeholders.

A "board" in this case can mean either a collection of volunteers or people with a financial stake in the business.

Either way, a recap email from a board meeting needs to condense a lot of information into a small space.

Subject line: Highlights from [month/year] [name of company/ organization] board meeting

Hi everyone,

Good morning/afternoon.

[Short intro; for instance, "The Acme Corporation board had a productive meeting on Tuesday, October 17. We made several decisions with respect to the company's staff and financials."]

Here are the highlights:

[Then, list off the highlights as bullet points and try to keep each bullet point to 1–2 sentences. For instance:

- "The auditor's report did not contain any observation or comments that have an adverse affect on the company.

- The board resolved to pay a dividend at the rate of 1% per year to be paid out of the current profits.

- Susan Williams, a director of the company, retired by rotation but offered herself for re-appointment. The board then re-appointed her a director of the company."]

[Finally, include any additional information; for instance, "I attached the full meeting minutes to this email."]

Please reach out with any comments/questions.

– Leader's first name

Email signature

Deeper Insight

Here, the leader needs to show his/her communication chops on two levels:

1. Take information from one group (board) and make it relevant for another group (ex: employees).

2. Distill the information down to an email that takes about two minutes to read.

In essence, the leader needs to demonstrate proper tone and convey a lot in a small space.

It's not an easy balance, but it's a necessary one.

HOW TO REPORT BACK TO SENIOR EXECUTIVES

If you're a manager with people above you, then you may often draft updates or reports to show your team's progress.

In the template below, let's focus on how to draft an email to superiors in which you tease highlights from a broader update or report.

Subject line: [The topic at hand; for instance, "July summary for Project Alpha"]

Hi [first names of the superiors or "team"],

Good morning/good afternoon.

I am passing along [the topic at hand; for instance, "July updates for Project Alpha. You can find a full report here."]

NOTE: the underlined is a hyperlink.

[Then summarize the main findings; for instance, "Below, I share three big takeaways and what's to come in August and September.

1. We found customers are 74% more likely to upgrade to our premium model if we lock in the rate for two years instead of one.

2. Takeaway #2 that can be explained in 1–2 sentences.

3. Takeaway #3 that can be explained in 1–2 sentences."]

[Then, explain next steps; for instance, "As we look ahead to August and September, our team plans to achieve the following:

1. Determine the impact of social media targeted advertising on past clients as a way to bring them back.

2. Next step #2 that can be explained in 1–2 sentences.

3. Next step #3 that can be explained in 1–2 sentences."]

If you have questions, please let me know.

Thanks,

– Leader's first name

Email signature

Deeper Insight

As a manager who oversees people below you and answers to people above, organizational skills are crucial.

You are in the middle and need your message heard on both ends.

Here, the email goes to higher-ups who may prefer the message is more like an executive summary. Yes, you can link them to deeper information, but the point is to share the main takeaways in a small space.

That's why it's important to use numbered or bulleted lists and condense each finding to 1–2 sentences.

Ask yourself, "If I only have 10 seconds to share a recent update, what would I say?" Then, write down the answer as a bullet point in the email.

As a manager with aspirations of working at the top levels of the company, your brief, focused emails will give a glimpse into your organizational skills.

Chapter 3
Write to Clients

Manage the relationship

Client relations is a delicate dance. Day after day, every word matters as you navigate a business relationship (new or old).

As a leader on the team, you must demonstrate poise and effective project management to the client — especially when projects go awry or the work becomes tangled (and perhaps a bit awkward).

On the following pages, you will find templates to help you with common client relations email scenarios. Each time, the template will help you look professional, courteous and on your game.

HOW TO REQUEST ADDITIONAL INFORMATION

Yes, clients hire you because you have a skillset they need. Still, your expertise doesn't mean you already know *everything* about the client's world too.

If you lead a graphic design company, you may still want a brief education on, for instance, civil engineering to design a marketing brochure for such a firm.

Don't be afraid to ask for more information, but always pose the question in terms of what you will do next.

Let's use the graphic design scenario for the template.

Subject line: Few additional questions about [task at hand; for instance, "the marketing brochure"]

Hi [client's first name],

Good morning/afternoon.

[Introduce your query; for instance, "As we design the marketing brochure, we have a few additional questions about your firm and the world of civil engineering, in general."]

If it's easier to answer these questions by phone, let me know.

[Lay out your questions one at a time. For instance:

   "1.   Are there any terms you need us to include in the brochure that are relevant to civil engineering or the clients you work with?

   2.   What fonts do you use on your website? We want to incorporate the same fonts in the brochure.

   3.   You mentioned it during our kickoff meeting, but what year did your grandfather begin the business?"]

[Explain how the work is already underway; for instance, "We have started on the brochure, and those three pieces of info will fill in the gaps so we can show you an initial draft, hopefully by next Monday."]

Thanks again,

– Leader's first name

Email signature

Deeper Insight

There are a few points to consider with the email:

1. The writer asks if a phone call might be easier. If you need a lot of additional information from the client, then a phone call is better than email. You will have a more efficient discussion on the phone in fifteen minutes than with nine back-and-forth emails over three hours.

2. The writer organizes the information through numbers (bullet points are also fine). Let the words breathe and allow the reader to answer each question one at a time.

3. Finally, the writer explains his/her team has already kicked off the project. Note the first three words ("As we design…"). The phrase makes the client feel like the project has momentum. It's a subtle way to say, "We're off and running."

Clients love to know you have everything under control. It makes them feel smart for hiring you.

HOW TO REPLY TO A REQUEST

Let's paint a picture. The client has a request that will take a bit of time to complete.

You see the email, process the amount of work that awaits you and have two choices.

1. Respond to the email and tell the client you will work on the request and provide an update soon.

2. Don't respond until you have completed the task.

Which one is best?

I will make the answer nice and clear. If you go with #1, you will make the client happy.

If you opt for #2, you will drive the client batty.

Answer as soon as possible with a confirmation of the request and a general timeline for the work you will complete. The approach puts the client at ease and shows you are a top-notch communicator.

Here's the template:

Hi [client's first name],

Thanks for your email. I received your request for [what the request entails; for instance, "the additional environmental study on the wetlands by February 17"].

[Provide the next steps; for instance, "Our team will begin on the study tomorrow and will keep you updated as we go along."]

If we have questions, I will be sure to reach out.

Have a great rest of the day,

– Leader's first name

Email signature

Deeper Insight

Never let the client wonder where you are. Ever.

Even if the request will take time to complete, answer right away and provide a status check.

You give the client peace of mind and the confidence to continue your working relationship.

HOW TO FOLLOW UP AFTER A MEETING OR CONVERSATION

After the client passes along new information or gives you a task, the best course of action is a follow-up email to reiterate what you are about to do.

As I wrote in the previous template (How to reply to a request), your goal is to give the client reassurance.

A recap email on what you will accomplish is one more way to look golden. Here's the template, short and sweet:

Subject line: Follow up from our conversation today

Hi [client's first name],

Thanks for the conversation today. To recap, my team and I will accomplish the tasks below in the coming [days/weeks/months].

[Then, share the action items in a bulleted or numbered list. For instance:

- Action item 1

- Action item 2

- Action item 3, etc.]

If I have questions, I will be sure to reach out.

[Provide any additional information about the process; for instance, "We can also go over any new information during our weekly check-in call. The next one is Monday, September 10 at 2 p.m. ET. I sent you a calendar invite for the check-in call."]

Thanks,

– Leader's first name

Email signature

Deeper Insight

There are two project management tips embedded in the template.

1. The action items are in bullet points so they are easy to read and understand. Include the bullet points so the client knows what you will work on. In case you leave something out or have info wrong, the client can respond and make corrections. Otherwise, you might spend time working in the wrong direction.

2. If the client engagement spans weeks or months, it's often smart to schedule regular check-in phone calls (ex: every week or every other week). In the template, the leader reminds the client of the next day/time for a call and also tells the client to look out for a calendar invite.

Always have a next step planned out. That's a mark of a true leader with respect to external communications.

HOW TO CLARIFY NEEDS OR SPECIFICATIONS

With client relations, never assume anything. A-N-Y-T-H-I-N-G.

If a client asks for help to design new business cards and you can't remember if she said bold font or not bold font for the name/title...

ASK. Simple as that.

Don't take chances or move too quickly. When in doubt, ASK.

Even tiny details — when done the wrong way — can cause enormous headaches for the client and diminish your standing in the relationship.

Here's a template that incorporates the business card scenario, to give you a real-life example.

Subject line: Quick question about [task at hand; for instance, "the business card design"]

Hi [client's first name],

[Give a status check; for instance, "We are working on your new business card design today and have a quick question."]

[Ask your question; for instance, "Do you want the name/title on the card to be **bolded** or not? I can't recall what we discussed."]

Please let me know,

– Leader's fist name

Email signature

Deeper Insight

Ask the simple, harmless question now and avoid all kinds of snafus and disgruntled client conversations later.

Imagine if the business cards went to the printer (5,000 copies—yikes!) and the name and title *weren't* supposed to be in bold. **Bad news.**

To be clear, you don't want to be the service provider who asks for a million clarifications. Listen the first time to avoid countless follow-up messages. But when you aren't 100% sure, ASK.

Your future self (and your future stress levels) will thank you.

Grow the relationship

HOW TO INVITE A CLIENT TO AN EVENT

Let's say your company plans a ribbon-cutting event for a new office space.

That means you want to invite your extended business network to celebrate (ex: current clients).

Yes, you might do an "evite" of some kind to collect RSVPs (ex: Facebook or other online event tool).

You should also consider separate messages to people like clients to add a personal touch. Always let clients know you're thinking about them.

Subject line: I hope you can attend the [your company name] [name of event]

Hi [client's first name] or [name of company] team,

Good morning/afternoon!

[Explain what happened; for instance, "This week, we sent an evite about the ribbon-cutting event for our new office on Tuesday, March 17 at 5:30 p.m."]

[Provide necessary details; for instance, "Our new address is 500 E. Main Street, and there's free parking."]

[Share additional details about the event and try to make it personal; for instance, "We will have food and drinks so come hungry. And today we finished a photo collage of past projects in the waiting area — you might see yourself on the wall from last year's Winter Gala!"]

Please let me know if you can make it.

– Leader's first name

Email signature

Deeper Insight

First of all, people can ignore a mass invite. But the personal touch in a separate email begs a response. If you want certain people to attend, go the extra mile.

Also note the "wrinkle" in the email, a tactic which makes the message authentic.

"And today we finished a photo collage of past projects in the waiting area — you might see yourself on the wall from last year's Winter Gala!"

No two emails are alike. This one is intended for a specific client with a connection to the "Winter Gala."

HOW TO CELEBRATE VICTORIES

When a client achieves a milestone, it's important that you, as a leader of your team, acknowledge the success.

Ultimately, if your client's business gains momentum, it could mean more work for you. But the decision to take a pause and congratulate someone else is a hallmark of strong leadership.

Subject line: Congrats on [the accomplishment; for instance, "Winning 'Best of the Best' Honors"]

Hi [client's first name],

[Explain what happened; for instance, "I saw in this week's *Local Business Today* that Acme Corporation was named 'Best of the Best' for IT firms in the region. Congrats on the award!"]

[Then, share what the accomplishment means to you; for instance, "We are proud to be your advertising partner and always appreciate the opportunity to work together."]

[Then, consider using the email to discuss next steps on a current project; for instance, "As a quick update, Jon and Stacy on our team will be in touch by the end of the week with new billboard options."]

Again, congrats on the award!

– Leader's first name

Email signature

Deeper Insight

Be clear about the "success" you reference in the email. Don't write, "Congrats on the award!" That's too vague. Note how the email above includes the name of the publication and the award itself.

And then consider using the email to update the client on your efforts ("new billboard options").

That way, you say "congrats" and show proof of your work.

That's a solid combination.

HOW TO INTRODUCE A CLIENT TO SOMEONE IN YOUR NETWORK

The best leaders help other people succeed.

They are always on alert for ways to connect clients, friends and colleagues. In doing so, they create interesting partnerships or, at a minimum, foster new conversations.

Never hesitate to look around your network and see how "your people" can benefit the client.

Subject line: Connecting two people who should know each other

Hi [your client's first name],

Good morning/afternoon.

I'd like you to meet [first and last name of the other person in your network].

[Other person's first name] is [job title and the person's role; for instance, "Sue Jenkins is vice president of development at Acme Bank"].

[Then, explain the nature of your message; for instance, "I know you mentioned the need to expand so you have more warehouse space and perhaps Sue could help with funding."]

[Provide information on the person you introduced into the conversation; for instance, "Sue is a good friend and Acme Bank helped our firm early on with renovation costs at our office."]

I cc'ed [name of person you introduced into the conversation; for instance, "Sue"] so feel free to respond and hopefully set up a conversation.

Good luck!

– Leader's first name

Email signature

Deeper Insight

It may be wise to ask your client if he/she wants a particular introduction before you send the email. Otherwise, you might put the client in an awkward spot and your goodwill gesture becomes anything but.

In general, it's a professional move to take time from a busy day and introduce two people you value.

Be the connector, and watch your own network become stronger!

HOW TO SEEK A CLIENT'S ADVICE

As I wrote in my first book, *Wait, How Do I Write This Email?*, a collection of writing templates for the job search and networking, people love to be asked to share what they know.

And the best subject line to stop busy people in their tracks includes the phrase, "need your advice."

Clients hire your company because you have knowledge and experience they lack. At the same time, your clients may possess a skillset *you* don't have.

A great way to deepen the relationship is to seek the client's wisdom.

Subject line: Need your advice on [task at hand; for instance, "501(c) (3) status"]

Hi [client's first name],

Good morning/good afternoon.

[The reason for your message; for instance, "Our company has floated the idea of starting a foundation as a more streamlined way to make charitable donations to worthy organizations here in the area.

I imagine your non-profit has 501(c)(3) status, right? If so, would you be able to hop on a conference call with our management team this week or next to share your experience setting up and managing a not-for-profit entity?"]

I know we would all benefit from your insights.

[Propose a next step; for instance, "We have availability on March 17, 18, 22 and 23. Do you have 20–30 minutes on any of those days?"]

Please let me know,

– Leader's first name

Email signature

Deeper Insight

The subject line, of course, contains "need your advice," which makes the reader feel valued right away.

The email then goes on to include, "we would all benefit from your insights." And the writer gives potential days for the conference call so the client doesn't blindly throw out available dates.

When you ask clients for advice, you draw them closer and show you respect what they have to say. The clients, in turn, appreciate you even more for seeking them out. Total win-win.

Provide various updates

HOW TO SHARE PROJECT MILESTONES OR DEVELOPMENTS

When you share project milestones or developments with clients, organization is a must.

For one, you want the client to understand all the great work you have accomplished.

And if you need clarification on a task, keep the message concise so the client can process the question and decide.

The template here includes both a milestone and a slight issue to show both sides of the coin.

Subject line: Latest with the [task at hand; for instance, "website development project"]

Hi [client's first name],

Good morning/afternoon.

[Give a status check; for instance, "We've made excellent progress on your new website and now have a home page mock-up for you to view. Click here to see the home page."]

[Then provide additional details in a bulleted or numbered list so the client can read each item. For instance:

"A few more updates:

- We have to make modifications to the video gallery feature and then we can show you the gallery likely on Friday morning.

- The site now displays properly on tablets. Before, the images appeared stretched out.

- Tammy Jones sent us her bio so we can finish out her page in the 'Meet the Team' area."]

[Finally, if you need the client's opinion or answer, set your question apart in its own paragraph so the client will see it; for instance, "One question for you: Do you want us to use the small or large Acme Corporation logo on each page? I think the small one is subtler, but I'll let you make the final call."]

Thanks,

– Leader's first name

Email signature

Deeper Insight

Share the biggest news first and then list off the other items as bullet points.

Finally, ask your question in a succinct manner. Keep the message tight and efficient so the client will read everything.

If you don't receive an answer to your question within 24 hours, follow back with:

"Hi there,

Please let me know you saw my question from yesterday about the size of the logo for your website. Thanks again."

Include the specific issue at hand ("size of the logo for your website") to jog the client's memory.

It's too vague to write, "Please let me know you saw my question from yesterday."

If you need an urgent response, pick up the phone and talk it out.

HOW TO CHECK IN AFTER TOO MUCH TIME HAS PASSED

Silence is a great way to damage a relationship with a client. When communication goes dark, clients begin to wonder, "Does this company even work for me anymore?"

When you feel too much time has gone by without an update, use the template below to share your efforts and regain the client's trust.

In the scenario below, a person who works for an event-planning business emails the client about the logistics for a client's company-wide event.

Subject line: Project updates to share

Hi [client's first name],

Good morning/afternoon.

[Set up the message; for instance, "We have several updates to pass along about your annual company summit. We're making progress and cleared a few major hurdles this week."]

[Then, provide each update in a bulleted or numbered list so the client can read the item. For instance:

- "The conference center team was able to give us an additional 100 chairs for the main session on Friday night.

- We have tested all the audio/visual equipment in the main ballroom and the four breakout rooms.

- The 'selfie station' for social media pictures will be set up and in place by Wednesday, February 17 — well in advance of people who arrive on Thursday morning."]

If you have questions right now, let me know. If you'd rather talk by phone, I am free [explain when you are available; for instance, "the rest of the afternoon"].

Let me know and thanks again,

– Leader's first name

Email signature

Deeper Insight

Put the updates in bullet form so they are easy to process.

And also make yourself available by phone. Don't act like the single email above is the only way you communicate with clients. If the client wants to talk by phone, then you do too.

Make yourself available and be accommodating (within reason). The client will appreciate it.

HOW TO TROUBLESHOOT A PROBLEM

When problems arise in a client relationship, it may be necessary for a leader in the company to step in and manage the issue.

That way, the client knows the company takes the situation seriously and will do whatever it takes to find a solution.

Here's a template to guide you:

Subject line: Update on [issue at hand; for instance, "Acme Office Chair 3000"]

Hi [client's first name],

Good morning/afternoon.

I'm [leader's first and last name], [job title; for instance, "vice president of customer relations] at [name of company or organization; for instance, "Acme Office Supply"].

NOTE: Job titles are lower case unless they precede the person's name. That's why the job title is written as "vice president of customer relations" and not "Vice President of Customer Relations" (see more capitalization rules on page 4).

[Then, provide context and update the client or customer on the issue; for instance, "I know you have been in contact with Heather and Brad on our team about the purchase of new office chairs. First, thank you for the business. We appreciate it.

Heather and Brad updated me on the issues with the chairs you received — the scratch marks on the arm rests and the stain on two of the seat cushions.

Of course, there is no cost to return the damaged chairs. I have expedited the shipment of new chairs, and they should arrive on Tuesday, June 23."]

[Finally, give a next step; for instance, "I will check back with you on Thursday, June 25 to make sure everything is resolved."]

NOTE: Be clear about any follow-up days or times. "Thursday, June 25" is much stronger than "sometime next week."

Thanks again for your patience and understanding.

– Leader's first name

Email signature

Deeper Insight

As a leader, you need to trust your instincts on when to supersede employees and take over. If you pull the move too much, it can undermine the relationship with people below you.

When done properly, the move can settle down upset clients/customers and make them feel like everything will work out in the end. Nobody expects perfection, but we demand excellent customer service in good times and bad.

Chapter 4
Same Message, Different Audiences

Introduction

A leader must tailor information to meet the needs of various stakeholders.

That's because some moments require a custom conversation versus a one-size-fits-all approach.

In Chapter 4, we break down how to share similar information with different groups and how the language should adapt each time.

Writing Scenario

Different audiences:

- Customers/clients
- Employees
- Donors/supporters

Scenario:

You run a software company and experience a data breach. Customer information is vulnerable, and your various audiences are all nervous but for different reasons.

Some people had sensitive personal data stolen (ex: clients). Others (ex: investors) worry about the long-term health of your business.

As the leader, every audience needs to hear from you. Time to start drafting emails.

CUSTOMERS/CLIENTS

Email to customers/clients

Subject line: Information about [issue at hand; for instance, "Acme Corporation data breach"]

Hi [person's first name, — that's if you can do a mass email and include names; otherwise, consider starting with the line below]

Good morning/afternoon.

I'm [leader's first and last name], the [job title; for instance, "CEO and founder"] at [name of company; for instance, "Acme Corporation"].

[Then, share the *news* right away. Don't bury the lead. For instance, "I'm writing to let you know Acme Corporation suffered a data breach on July 21. We know the breach impacted 32,000 of our 3.2 million customers and that a person's name, address and credit card information were compromised."]

[Next, provide your takeaway on the *news* and your company's next steps; for instance, "We take pride in our security protocols and have redoubled efforts to make sure your information is secure. We are sorry the breach occurred and know we need to work even harder to regain your trust."]

[Then, explain the next steps for the client. For instance:

"Please follow the short checklist below to make sure your account is protected:

1. Go here to update your password.

2. We have provided one year of credit monitoring for free through our partner, Acme Credit Check. Go here to request the service.

3. Check your credit card statements for any fraudulent charges.]

[Finally, wrap up the message with a sense of confidence. For instance:

"As a customer of Acme Corporation, we value your trust above all else. We know we damaged that trust with the data breach.

We will work hard to fix the breach and ensure one doesn't happen again. And we hope you will remain part of the Acme Corporation family."]

Thanks for your business,

– Leader's first name

Job title

Name of company

Deeper Insight

In the example above, the leader has to share bad news with customers. Not every email will be so heavy (data breach).

In any event, it's critical to provide the main piece of information right up front. Don't leave the "meat" of the email (the data breach occurred) until the end.

Then, be sure to explain next steps as a result of the news and any action items for the reader.

When you have news to share with customers/clients, you must be:
— Brief
— Straightforward
— Clear about what comes next

What to avoid:
— Don't make jokes or light of a situation. Even if the nature of the email is positive, people interpret tone 1,000 different ways in an email. Play it right down the middle.

— Don't go on too long. Make your point, give a call to action and get out of someone's inbox.

— Don't seem flippant or unsympathetic. The first thing the reader will think is, "Oh, he's the rich boss disconnected from the rest of us. He doesn't care what we're going through."

In the next template, we examine a leader's email about the data breach intended for the employees of Acme Corporation.

EMPLOYEES

Email to employees

Subject line: Information about [issue at hand; for instance, "Acme Corporation data breach"]

Hi team,

Good morning/afternoon.

I'm writing to let you know [be up front with the *news*; for instance, "Acme Corporation suffered a data breach on July 21. We know the breach impacted 32,000 of our 3.2 million customers and that a person's name, address and credit card information were compromised."]

[Next, share your takeaway on the *news* and your company's next steps; for instance, "As you know, we take pride in our security protocols and have redoubled efforts to make sure customer information is secure. Jon Vergara, our COO, is working around the clock with our technical team to secure the network and make certain no additional customer information is stolen."]

[Then, explain how employees should handle the issue at hand when speaking to clients/customers; for instance, "If customers ask you about the data breach, please refer them to this page for information on how to protect customer information, update passwords and seek free credit monitoring for up to one year."]

[Finally, wrap up the message with any other calls to action and a confident tone; for instance, "If you have specific questions about the data breach, direct them to Jon Vergara at jvergara@acmecorporation.com.

Thanks for your hard work and dedication during this critical time."]

– Leader's first name

Job title

Name of company

Deeper Insight

In the template, the leader must put forth news of the data breach with employees. Like the template to customers/clients, the approach is the same: brief, straightforward and clear about what comes next.

Yes, the message is to the leader's own team so the relationship is more casual than with a paying customer. But the tone needs to remain professional — especially when the topic is serious.

Also note how the leader has delegated and empowered the COO to spearhead the effort to secure the company's sensitive information. Yes, the leader is in charge, but that doesn't mean he/she needs to do everything.

Jon Vergara, in this case, has greater experience with network security and he's the COO. He should be the point person. The leader needs to play to the team's strengths and let others take control when appropriate. The strategy isn't passing the buck; it's drawing upon the collective brainpower of the people on staff.

Whether something went well (ex: company won a distinction) or it's the "worst week ever" (ex: data breach), your emails must command respect and make employees feel you're in control.

It's often said in sports that players take on the mentality of their coaches. Every email you send your team dictates how they, in turn, approach their work.

In the final template, we examine how the leader shares the data breach information with donors/supporters.

DONORS/SUPPORTERS

Email to donors/supporters

Subject line: Information about [issue at hand; for instance, "Acme Corporation data breach"]

Hi everyone,

Good morning/afternoon.

I'm writing to let you know [be up front with the *news*; for instance, "Acme Corporation suffered a data breach on July 21. We know the breach impacted 32,000 of our 3.2 million customers and that a person's name, address and credit card information were compromised."]

[Next, share your takeaway on the *news* and your company's next steps; for instance, "As you know, we take pride in our security protocols and have redoubled efforts to make sure customer information is secure. Jon Vergara, our COO, is working around the clock with our technical team to secure the network and ensure no additional customer information is stolen."]

[Then, make the case your company is still worth someone's investment; for instance, "Yes, this is a difficult time for our company, but we will emerge from the experience stronger and more capable than ever."]

[Finally, wrap up the message with a thank you; for instance, "If you have specific questions about the data breach, direct them to Jon Vergara at jvergara@acmecorporation.com.

Thank you, as always, for your support."]

– Leader's first name

Job title

Name of company

_____

Deeper Insight

If your organization has donors (ex: nonprofit) or you relied on supporters to launch a project (ex: crowdfunding), you may feel compelled to send an email like the one here.

Above all, the leader needs to send an email to donors or supporters early on so rumors don't spread. Stay in front of a tricky situation; don't run and hide.

Chapter 5
Network Like a Leader

Common Situations

HOW TO CONNECT TWO PEOPLE WITHIN YOUR COMPANY/ ORGANIZATION

A leader should be a master connector — someone who has a birds-eye view of the company/organization and always looks to create new relationships to drive the business forward.

If you see an opportunity to introduce one employee to another — perhaps people in different divisions who could collaborate or learn from each other — then draft the email and make it happen.

Subject line: Two [name of company/organization] team members who should meet

Hi [first name of employee A and first name of employee B],

Good morning/afternoon.

As we [the task or initiative at hand; for instance; "move into the eco-friendly products space"], I think it would be smart for you to meet each other and collaborate.

[First and last name of employee A] is [describe the person; for instance, "new to our marketing division and oversees our social media campaigns"].

[First and last name of employee B] is [describe the person; for instance, "a veteran of our products division and has spearheaded our eco-friendly efforts"].

Please find time to meet, make introductions and [explain what you want the two people to do; for instance, "knock around ideas on the best ways to promote our new products on social media"].

Keep me cc'ed on the email chain so I know when/where the meeting will happen.

Thanks,

– Leader's first name

Email signature

Deeper Insight

If you see an opportunity to connect employees for a strategic purpose, then do it. The conversation can only help to evolve the business and sharpen your capabilities.

Also note how the leader asks to be cc'ed on the email chain. That way, the leader is still "watching" (so to speak) to make sure the employees follow through on the meeting.

And since the leader knows when the meeting takes place, he/she can check back on the two employees afterward (if necessary) to see if any interesting ideas emerged.

HOW TO CONNECT AN EMPLOYEE WITH SOMEONE OUTSIDE THE COMPANY/ORGANIZATION

As we discussed in the previous template (How to connect two people within your company/organization), a leader should always have a "big picture" view of the business and spark conversations among the right people.

That same mentality extends to developing relationships between employees and people outside of the business.

It's often helpful for the leader to kickstart a conversation and then step back to let the employee take over.

Subject line: Connecting with [name of person outside the company/ organization]

Hi [first name of employee],

Good morning/afternoon.

I have cc'ed [first and last name of person outside the company/organization] to this email. [Explain the nature of the relationship; for instance, "I met her at the recent happy hour hosted by the Charlotte Business Network."]

[First and last name of person outside the company/organization] is [describe the person briefly; for instance, "a freelance writer who expressed interest in our new Top Dog profile series on pets and their owners who use our pet products."]

[First name of person outside the company/organization], I connected you with [first and last name of employee] because [explain the employee's role; for instance, "she manages our editorial team"].

[First name of employee], please respond back with a time you are free to chat with [first name of person outside the company/organization]. Keep me cc'ed on the email chain so I stay in the loop.

Thanks,

– Leader's first name

Email signature

Deeper Insight

There are countless reasons to connect an employee with someone from the outside business world.

Each time, make it clear to your employee the nature of the email ("expressed interest in our new Top Dog profile series"). Context is important so the employee doesn't think, "What does my boss want me to do with this person?"

Jump start the meeting and then allow your employee to assess the value of the new person. That's a great way to be a leader and delegate at the same time.

HOW TO SEEK ADVICE FROM ANOTHER LEADER

The best leaders know they can always improve. That's why it's important to maintain a healthy network of other leaders and seek out those people for advice when appropriate.

Benefit from someone else's viewpoint, and you will strengthen your own leadership ability.

As I discussed earlier in the book, the best way to capture the attention of a busy person is to use three special words in the subject line: **Need your advice.**

Subject line: Need your advice about [task at hand; for instance, "staffing decisions"]

Hi [first name of the other leader],

Good morning/afternoon.

96

[Then, one line of small talk to open the conversation; for instance, "How is business since your expansion with the new office? Has the craziness settled down?"]

I'm reaching out because [explain what you want from the person; for instance, "I need your advice as I decide on how to manage my team and delegate responsibilities.

I think I want to create team leads within each division and would value your perspective on the best ways to empower the people I select as leads"].

Do you have a few minutes to chat this week? [Then, give the person a day that's best; for instance, "I'm pretty open on Friday if that works for you."]

Please let me know,

– Leader's first name

Email signature

Deeper Insight

Raise your hand if you feel important when someone asks for your advice. Exactly.

And in the email above, the leader is careful to explain the nature of the request so the reader doesn't think, "What the heck are we going to talk about?" People need context before they can act.

From a networking perspective, it's also smart to seek counsel from a fellow leader. The move brings your network closer and keeps your business top of mind with other decision makers.

Finally, the email is designed to set up a phone call. Don't glean wisdom from someone else entirely over email. You will gain much more through a phone call (or coffee chat) because of the real-time conversation.

HOW TO DEVELOP A PARTNERSHIP

I mentioned in the previous template (How to seek advice from another leader) that it's important to maintain a strong network.

One reason is the opportunity to develop partnerships with people (and their companies) you respect.

Here's an example between the owner of a health foods store and the owner of a tea company.

Subject line: Potential partnership idea with [name of your company/ organization]

Hi [first name of leader at other company/organization],

Good morning/afternoon.

[Start off with a little small talk; for instance, "How did your team fare on Small Business Saturday? We had decent in-store traffic during the morning, but it tapered off by afternoon."]

I'm reaching out to explore a possible partnership. [Explain the reason for the partnership request; for instance, "We had great feedback when you provided samples of your green tea in our store."]

[Then, share a possible next step; for instance, "Would you like to set up a display with the tea? I want to see how the product does in our beverage area."]

Please let me know when we can talk about the idea further. [Provide your availability; for instance, "I'm free Thursday morning if that works for you."]

Thanks,

– Leader's first name

Email signature

Deeper Insight

Note how the writer cuts to the chase in the second section ("I'm reaching out to explore a possible partnership"). Always put your "bottom line up front," a concept we explore in *Wait, How Do I Promote My Business?*, my collection of writing guides for startups and small businesses.

The email also includes a clear example of a partnership or business deal ("set up a display").

The reader has all the information to make an informed decision in the email reply.

HOW TO FOLLOW UP WITH A KEY PERSON FROM A CONFERENCE

Leaders attend conferences to learn, grow and meet new people.

And if you come across someone interesting who can advance your business, it's important to send a message when you're back at your desk to keep the dialogue going.

Here's how:

Subject line: Great to meet you at [name of event/conference; for instance, "BizCon 2000"]

Hi [person's first name],

I'm [your first and last name] with [name of company].

It was nice to meet you at [name of event/conference]. I enjoyed learning more about [what you gleaned from the other person; for instance, "the work you do at Acme Corporation related to finance and accounting. Plus, I needed someone to joke with during that boring keynote address"].

Let's keep the discussion going. [Then, the next step; for instance, "As I mentioned, our company is looking for a new accounting firm and yours may be a good fit. I will connect you with our CFO in a separate email so you two can meet."]

Thanks again,

– Leader's first name

Email signature

___

Deeper Insight

Put the name of the event/conference where you met in the subject line (ex: BizCon 2000). The proper noun makes your email more recognizable in a crowded inbox.

Also, make sure to explain the next step ("looking for a new accounting firm"). The person may not want to follow up if he/she doesn't know the "why."

HOW TO BRING IN A GUEST/MOTIVATIONAL SPEAKER

Professional development is the lifeblood of a strong company/organization. Employees always need to find ways to improve, and it's useful to learn from outside voices.

If you want to employ the services of a guest/motivational speaker, send a succinct email that explains your intentions.

___

Subject line: Interest in [name of speaker] addressing the team at [name of company/organization]

Hi [first name of speaker],

Good morning/afternoon.

I'm [your first and last name], a/an/the [job title] at [name of company/organization]. I hope you're doing well.

[Explain the nature of your message; for instance, "We have a professional development series and like to bring in engaging speakers who give our employees new perspectives."]

[Explain how you came across the speaker; for instance, "I watched a few of your online videos on team building and think you have a great presentation style."]

What is your availability [give some options; for instance, "in November or December? Our professional development sessions are 90 minutes long."]

I look forward to hearing from you,

– Leader's first name

Email signature

Deeper Insight

Make your subject line descriptive and include the name of your company so the message stands out.

Also, be specific with how you located the person. Everyone wants to know how someone else discovered their business so save the person from having to ask, "How did you find me?"

Use the email to see if the speaker is available. Then, set up a phone call to discuss the parameters of the event.

HOW TO ASK SOMEONE TO MAKE AN INTRODUCTION ON YOUR BEHALF

Often the best way to meet a business contact is through a mutual friend or colleague.

The "connector" person can open the door through an email introduction, but you, as a leader of your company/organization, should help the person and provide details for the intro email.

Here's how:

Subject line: Connecting me with [first and last name of the person you want to meet]

Hi [first name of your friend/colleague],

Good morning/afternoon.

Thanks again for connecting me with [first and last name of the person you want to meet]. I appreciate the intro. I included language below you can use.

If you need additional info, let me know.

> *NOTE: The information below is a template for a mock email the person can send to introduce you.*

Possible subject line: Connecting you with [your first and last name] from [name of your company]

I'm introducing you to [your first and last name; for instance, Reese Bowers"], a/an/the [job title] at [name of company].

[Then, the reason for the introduction; for instance, "Reese leads a division at Acme Corporation that develops virtual reality tools to help people overcome phobias like a fear of heights.

I know you manage a large mental health clinic here in Boston so I thought you two might be able to help each other."]

[Then include a link to your work so your connector doesn't have to search for one; for instance, "You can see examples of the virtual reality tools here."]

Deeper Insight

Let the connector write the email intro and ending with his/her own small talk. Remember, your job here is to provide the "guts" of the email with info on the work you do, the reason for meeting the new person and a link to your work.

Your friend/colleague will take your language and customize it.

HOW TO STAY IN TOUCH WITH YOUR NETWORK

A network is a group of people who remain in your personal and professional orbit *all your life*.

We pick up new friends and colleagues year over year. We may not stay in touch on a regular basis, but some moments require us to check back in.

Examples of appropriate times to update your network:

▸ Start a new job

▸ Land a promotion

▸ Earn an accomplishment

▸ Seek new people to hire

▸ Update on a new hire

▸ Help someone else find a job or new opportunity

You may need to contact one person from your network, one group of people within your network or every darn person you've come across.

Whoever it is, the structure of the email remains the same.

▸ Make introductions

▸ Explain the nature of your message

▸ Provide supporting information

▸ Close it out

103

Below, let's explore emails in which we connect with one person, a specific group and a large group.

How to stay in touch with one person from your network

Scenario: A friend recommended a person for a job at your company. In the end, the person landed the job. Now you send a message to the friend about the news.

Subject line: Update on [task at hand; for instance, "filling our new project manager role"]

Hi [person's first name],

I hope all is well. [Then, a line of small talk the person will appreciate; for instance, "How is it going at the new gig? Are you getting used to your role as senior VP?"]

[Then, explain right away the nature of your message; for instance, "I'm writing to let you know we did end up hiring Dee Folsom, the person you recommended a few months back, as our new project manager."]

[Next, provide a bit more information on the news; for instance, "Dee was originally a finalist for the role, and we went with someone else. Then the other person ultimately was not the best fit. We asked Dee if she was still interested and she was."]

[Finally, wrap up the message; for instance, "Thanks again for the recommendation. Huge help! Please let me know if I can ever return the favor."]

Thanks,

– Leader's first name

Email signature

Deeper Insight

Start off with a question about the other person. Show you want to know the latest about him/her.

Then, share the news and provide background. Ask yourself, "What questions might the person have once I provide the information?" Do your best to fill in the gaps (ex: we hired Dee, and here's how it went down).

At best, the email strengthens your network by keeping "your people" close. At worst, the email makes the other person feel good because he/she knows the favor led to something great.

Either way, drafting the message is time well spent.

———

How to stay in touch with a specific group from your network

Scenario: You need to hire a new director of analytics at your company. You reach out to an email list of brothers from your college fraternity to see if anyone has a recommendation.

Subject line: [Task at hand; for instance, "Looking for a new director of analytics"]

Hi everyone,

I hope all is well. [Then, a line of small talk the group will appreciate; for instance, "I was at the fraternity house last month for homecoming. Great to see several of you — and good to know the house is still standing!"]

[Then, explain right away the nature of your message; for instance, "My company, Acme Corporation, is looking for a new director of analytics. See the full job posting here. I'm curious if anyone has a solid recommendation."]

[Next, provide a bit more information on the news; for instance, "The applicants need to have at least three years in the data analytics space. If they have done work in the medical field, even better."]

[Finally, wrap up the message; for instance, "Again, let me know if you have someone in mind."]

Thanks,

– Leader's first name

Email signature

Deeper Insight

Kick off the message with a reference the entire group will appreciate. I used the example, "the house is still standing!"

Then, share news or make a request in the next section. Don't force the readers to hunt around for the point of your message.

Recognize you have popped up in the inboxes of people you might not talk to that often. Be conversational but cut to the chase and see who responds.

How to stay in touch with a large group from your network

Scenario: You start a new job and want your crowd to know. You also use the opportunity to explain your business in case there are ways to work together.

Subject line: [Task at hand; for instance, "Update on my new job"]

Hi everyone,

I hope all is well with each of you.

[Then, explain right away the nature of your message; for instance, "I'm writing to let you know I have started a new chapter in my career as the director of sales for Acme Corporation.

I enjoyed my last three years as a junior sales associate at Tech Corporation, and I'm excited to make the jump to director at a new company."]

[Next, provide a bit more information on the news; for instance, "Acme Corporation is a leader across the Midwest for industrial farming equipment. Here's a look at our product catalog."]

[Then, give people a way to engage; for instance, "If you are in the market for equipment, please reach out. My new email is shelly@acmecorporation. com and my direct line is 555-555-5555."]

[Finally, wrap up the message; for instance, "If you have any career updates, I'd love to know. Reply to the message and catch me up."]

Thanks,

– Leader's first name

Email signature

Deeper Insight

Since the email goes out to such a diverse group, you can't incorporate small talk as easily. I recommend you leave it out.

Instead, jump right into your news. Provide links when necessary and give people context around the information. Never assume the reader knows the kind of work you do. Start from square one ("Acme Corporation is a leader across the Midwest for industrial farming equipment"). Many people won't know what the company does by its name alone.

At the end, ask anyone else to share career updates too. Networking is a two-way street. Plus, if other people provide highlights, it might spur new ways to work together.

HOW TO LEAVE SOMEONE A POSITIVE REVIEW

Clients or colleagues may ask you to give them an online review (ex: on Google or an industry-specific website). In those moments, your words have a chance to elevate someone else's business.

The goal is to take your review from standard to special. Here's how:

> [Open with why you appreciate the person or company's efforts; for instance, "Acme Corporation did a great job with our 2019 financial audit."]

> [Then, take the review deeper and explain *why* you felt the person or company performed well and include details; for instance, "We brought in the Acme team a bit late in the year, but they jumped into action and completed the audit by the deadline."]

> [Then, consider an even more specific example of the person or company's effort; for instance, "Special thanks to Frank Griffin of Acme Corporation for his diligence to find missing pieces of our financial history and make sure the audit was 100% complete."]

> [Finally, encourage others to use the person or company; for instance, "I believe all firms in need of a financial audit should work with Acme Corporation. They make the process easy!"]

Deeper Insight

Try hard to share moments from the experience with the person or company ("Special thanks to Frank Griffin"). It will make your review more believable and authentic.

Yes, it will require another 30 seconds to share a highlight from the relationship, but the gesture will mean a great deal more to the person who asked you to write the review.

Chapter 6
Handwritten Thank-You Notes

A handwritten note from a leader is pure class.

The move says, "Yes, I am busy and have many responsibilities, but I always have time to recognize someone else's hard work."

I recommend you have thank-you notes at your desk with letterhead that reads, "From the desk of [your first and last name]." Then, when the opportunity arises to write someone, you only need to pull a blank note from your drawer, grab a pen and go.

Remember to use blue or black ink (anything else is unprofessional) and put the date in the top right.

Common Situations

HOW TO THANK AN EMPLOYEE FOR A JOB WELL DONE

[Employee's first name],   Month Day, Year

Thanks for your efforts to [what the person did and why the task was significant; for instance, "spearhead our company-wide day of community service. I know we put a lot on your plate with five different community service locations at the same time, but the event was a big success"].

[Then, share one example of why the employee's hard work stood out; for instance, "I loved the group photo of our team at the Acme Homeless Shelter. Days like this build team spirit and make us stronger as a unit."]

Keep up the great work,

                           – Leader's first name

Deeper Insight

Could you write the same message in an email? Sure. But does the handwritten note mean more? No doubt.

As a leader, you should always think about long-term reputation and legacy. The employee might be so touched that he/she keeps the note in a desk drawer or somewhere else for safekeeping.

The little stuff means a lot, especially for people who work hard on your team.

HOW TO THANK A CLIENT FOR AN OPPORTUNITY

When a client helps you open a door (or perhaps you're grateful for the client relationship, in general), a handwritten note is the best course of action.

Never let a good opportunity go by to demonstrate your professionalism.

[Client's first name],   Month Day, Year

[Explain what happened and why it was significant; for instance, "Thank you again for introducing us to Dave Walls. He's an excellent photographer and did a fantastic job with our employee headshots and capturing our summer retreat.

Plus, Dave needs a new website and hired our firm to design it for him. It's a win-win all the way around."]

Thanks again for your help and for being a great client!

– Leader's first name

Deeper Insight

Make sure to tell the client how the help or favor made an impact (ex: "fantastic job with our employee headshots").

The details will mean more than a simple line like, "Thanks for recommending Dave Walls!"

If you're going through the effort to draft a handwritten note, then take it all the way and create a message that's one of a kind.

HOW TO THANK SOMEONE FOR A BUSINESS REFERRAL

When a person in your business network refers you to a new client, then a handwritten note is in order.

An email thank-you note is courteous, but paper and pen say, "This referral means the world to me." And as a leader, the handwritten message speaks volumes about the quality of your entire team.

[Person's first name],   Month Day, Year

Thank you so much for connecting me with [name of new client's first and last name; for instance, "Gina Solomon"] at [name of client's company; for instance, "Acme Corporation"]. [Then, explain what happened; for instance, "Gina has hired us to do the landscaping for Acme's new headquarters. Your referral was key to the new relationship."] Thank you for thinking of our team and trusting our abilities. If I can ever return the favor, let me know.

                         – Leader's first name

Deeper Insight

Be sure to tell your "connector" friend what happened ("Gina has hired us... landscaping"). Make sure the friend knows what became of the referral.

And remember to write, "If I can ever return the favor, let me know." Networking and referrals are a two-way street.

HOW TO THANK SOMEONE WHO WENT ABOVE AND BEYOND

A thank-you note is a must when someone goes the extra mile for you or your team.

Leaders need to spotlight when other people do more than expected.

[Person's first name],   Month Day, Year

Thank you for [what the person did; for instance, "putting in the extra hours over last weekend to finish out the remodel of our office kitchen"].

[Then explain why the extra effort means a lot; for instance, "Everyone is excited for the new kitchen, and we threw a little celebration when we walked in Monday morning to find everything done."]

[Then wrap up the note, perhaps with a final endorsement of the person's effort; for instance, "I will be sure to recommend your company if other people ask me about kitchen renovations."]

Thanks again,

– Leader's first name

Deeper Insight

Details make a handwritten note unforgettable. See how the note includes the line, "…we threw a little celebration when we walked in Monday morning." That kind of visual makes the recipient feel like a million bucks.

When people do a great job, they should be recognized. As a leader on your team, it's your responsibility to make it happen.

HOW TO COMPOSE A FORMAL LETTER

Some moments require a leader to step away from the inbox and draft a formal letter.

Here are a few instances where letter writing makes sense:

- Send a note of congratulations

- Share condolences

- Congratulate an employee

- Thank a client

- Incorporate as part of a holiday gift

To be clear, a letter is different than a handwritten note. The document usually contains a company's letterhead (logo, address and contact information).

FOR EXAMPLE:

COMPANY LOGO

ADDRESS

CONTACT INFORMATION

Dear Mr./Ms. [last name],

[The message]

Sincerely,

– Leader's first and last name

[Then, the leader's signature in blue or black pen]

It's a classy move to take a pause from a busy day and draft a letter on paper. You might even walk into a client's office one day and see your letter framed on the wall.

Letter writing is so rare these days that the document becomes commemorative and a treasure.

Imagine how you can make someone else feel.

Chapter 7
LinkedIn for Leaders

Write a powerful profile

INTRODUCTION

LinkedIn is the world's professional networking playground. Anyone who's anyone is on the site with a spiffy profile and headshot.

How can you, as a leader of your team, position yourself on LinkedIn so you look polished and professional?

On the following pages, you will find templates for different sections of a LinkedIn profile. I have done similar templates for jobseekers in *Wait, How Do I Write This Email?* and entrepreneurs in *Wait, How Do I Promote My Business?*

Now we focus on LinkedIn for leadership. Let's dive in.

PROFESSIONAL HEADLINE

Right below your headshot and name, LinkedIn asks you to create a professional headline.

Most people write their job title as the headline:

President, Acme Corporation

I recognize there's value in leading with your job title if you are in a position of authority. It carries weight to tell people right away you are a "president" or "vice president" or "division manager."

But consider a different approach. What if you used the professional headline as a way to connote the value your company provides (AKA the difference you make in the world)?

What if the headline looked like:

Improving healthcare one patient at a time (Instead of: COO, Acme Health System)

Or perhaps:

Tampa's pest control expert (Instead of: President, Acme Pest Control)

You know your business best. Think about your value proposition and why someone should contact you (ex: Tampa's pest control expert). And then consider how you can translate that value into a professional headline in eight or fewer words. Any longer and you might lose the reader's attention.

Even though you are in management, there are thousands if not millions of people on LinkedIn with the same job title.

A unique professional headline will help you stand out if someone is scrolling a list of names and faces. The headline will make the person stop, ponder a bit and perhaps click on your profile.

What good is social media if we don't use it to stand out?

PROFILE SUMMARY

I have developed a formula for a LinkedIn profile summary that's applicable to job seekers and entrepreneurs.

It's a three-step process that allows anyone, through a short paragraph, to describe who they are, what they do and why their work matters.

The same approach applies to leaders.

In fact, it's even more essential for leaders to articulate their purpose and value in a small space. Brevity and clarity are hallmarks of effective communication as we discussed in Chapter 1 called the Writing Master Class for Leaders (page 3).

Let's break down the three steps of a LinkedIn profile summary.

Step 1: Who are you, really?

You are more than a "president," "manager" or "CFO." What is your purpose on the team, and what value do you bring every day?

Step 2: What do you do?

Take the reader inside your world and share two to three details of your work. Let people visualize your role and gain a clearer picture of the product or service you provide.

Step 3: Bring 'em home

Ask yourself: why do I wake up each day, go to work and do what I do? What's the point? What's it all about? Determine the reason and add the sentence at the end.

Then, you have created a compact profile summary that draws people in and relays the importance of your job.

Here's a mock LinkedIn profile for a leader that follows the three-step formula.

Step 1: Who are you, really?

I'm a senior director at Acme Financial Services, a wealth management firm in Duluth, Minnesota.

We help hundreds of people across Minnesota make sound investment decisions so they can live comfortably today and plan for tomorrow.

NOTE: In two sentences, we learn what the person does and why the work matters. That's a great first step as someone "meets us" on LinkedIn.

Step 2: What do you do?

At Acme Financial, I manage a team of nine financial planners and serve clients of my own. We make sure clients receive one-on-one attention as they explore investments options and 401(k) plans.

I also contribute a monthly column to *Business Weekly* magazine on smart investments and financial strategies.

NOTE: Here, we go deeper with specific keywords like investments and 401(k). Why?

1. *People might search on LinkedIn by keyword so make sure the words specific to your business are in the profile summary.*

2. *Specific, detail-rich language is better writing and more enjoyable to read.*

Step 3: Bring 'em home

My goal is to give clients peace of mind and the confidence to build the lives they want for themselves and their families.

NOTE: In the last section, we need to ask ourselves: what is my career all about, and how do I make others better?

You may even want to discuss your "why" as a team and understand each employee's answer to the question.

Then, add step 3 to the LinkedIn profile and you're all set.

OTHER WORDS THAN "MANAGE" OR "LEAD"

When you write about work experience as a leader, it can be easy to fall into a routine with verb usage.

- **Manage** a team of 17 people in Acme Corporation's Atlanta office

- **Lead** a division that creates eco-friendly cleaning products

- **Manage** the company's social media channels on Twitter and Facebook

- **Lead** the...

You get the idea. "Manage" and "lead" are strong verbs, but they become stale when overused. What other verbs could we choose?

Here are several options:

▸ Oversee

▸ Direct

▸ Supervise

▸ Run

▸ Head

▸ Steer

▸ Guide

In general, it's important to watch out for duplicates. In other words, don't use the same word (ex: noun or verb) more than once in a sentence or even a paragraph. Your writing will be more colorful and varied if you mix up the word choice.

Here's an example with duplicate verbs.

*As vice president of Acme Corporation, I **manage** 17 people in our Atlanta office. As well, I **lead** a division that creates eco-friendly cleaning products and **manage** our social media channels on Twitter and Facebook.*

Now here's the same paragraph with different verbs each time.

*As vice president of Acme Corporation, I **manage** 17 people in our Atlanta office. As well, I **lead** a division that creates eco-friendly cleaning products and **oversee** our social media channels on Twitter and Facebook.*

Only one word is different now (**oversee** instead of **manage**). But doesn't the second version feel a little more professional?

As I often say, the details make the difference. Avoiding duplicates is a classic example.

QUANTIFY YOUR IMPACT

As you fill in the Work Experience area on LinkedIn, it's critical to keep the "q" word at front of your mind.

That's right. **Quantify**.

No matter the experience or accomplishment, you must ask yourself three questions:

- How many?

- How much?

- How often?

No, you didn't add "several new clients" in the most recent calendar year.

You "added eight new clients." **(How many?)** And you helped one of the clients coordinate a fundraiser that raised $250,000. **(How much?)**

And to raise the $250,000, you didn't "stage a large-scale social media campaign that reached a wide audience."

No, you "staged a two-month Facebook campaign **(How often?)** that reached 750,000 people **(How many?)** and generated 2,452 new fans of the client's Facebook business page **(How many?)**. The social media traction alone raised $43,000 **(How much?)** before the fundraiser took place."

How can you quantify the work of your team? As a leader, dig into the data and find the statistics that speak to the impact.

If you need to go around and ask team members to locate certain numbers, that's OK. It's worth the extra effort because data tells the story. And, as the expression goes, "numbers don't lie."

Outreach messages

HOW LEADERS SEND CONNECTION REQUESTS

Do you remember the last person who sent you a LinkedIn connection request?

...Are you still thinking about it?

The reason you can't remember is because the person likely did not attach a note. Without a note, the connection request is one more name floating through the social network's ecosystem.

As a leader, your modus operandi is to be memorable and distinguishable at every turn.

You have a golden opportunity to stand out with every new LinkedIn connection request. Why? Three reasons.

1. The best leaders do more than people expect. We touch on examples of the concept (Underpromise and Overdeliver) on page 145. When a LinkedIn request contains a note, it catches people by surprise — in a good way.

2. A short, authentic message with a LinkedIn request helps to build a relationship before the conversation even starts. Your words could spur a response from the other person and lead to a dialogue.

3. The extra effort can showcase your managerial chops. The message proves you know how to carry yourself as a leader and be a public face of your business.

Examples:

Reference a specific example from the person's work to make the outreach authentic.

"I read your blog post on smart leadership in the digital age and thought I'd connect to follow more of your LinkedIn content. I agree with your point about less screen time during in-person staff meetings. Keep up the great writing."

Follow up if you met the person at an event and be sure to include an example from your shared experience.

"It was great to meet you at the Downtown Young Leaders Happy Hour. I hope by now the conference center has fixed the blown speakers (my ears are still ringing). Let's keep in touch."

Use the space to ask a question. Then the person may respond, and you could enter into a discussion within minutes.

"I enjoyed your talk on the 'Acme Smart Money' podcast and especially the part about assessing the financial health of your company. I'd like to explore your services for my team. Do you have availability in October?"

Take an extra 20 seconds, draft a special message and make sure you are *never* "just another leader" with a LinkedIn account.

If you believe you have something special inside and can go further than your peers, then prove it through your actions.

Custom LinkedIn requests are a great place to start.

HOW LEADERS CRAFT NETWORKING MESSAGES

Too often, people view LinkedIn as a tool only necessary for the job search.

Not so.

LinkedIn offers limitless networking opportunities and the chance to start conversations with people in your space.

As a leader, you should make LinkedIn a main part of your toolkit. And when it's time to craft a networking message, consider the strategies below.

▸ Customization is critical

You are a leader. That means you need to hold yourself to a higher standard. Don't send out generic, cookie-cutter messages that feel impersonal as we discussed on the previous pages.

Here's one more example:

"Hi, I was checking out your terrific company and would love to connect!"

Sure, I bet you write that to *all* the companies. Here's a better version:

"Hi Stephanie, I spent time on your website learning about the latest advancements in diabetes research, especially with Project Alpha.

We are working on a project that might complement your efforts. It's a data insights tool that tracks someone's eating and exercise routines.

Perhaps we can talk further about it?"

Time to write the generic message: five seconds.

Time to write the personal message: 30 seconds.

Can you find 25 extra seconds to make your writing authentic — and stand a greater chance at a response? I bet you can.

▶ Name-drop like a savvy vet

When you couple the person's name with actual facts about his/her business (like we did above), your approach becomes genuine and undeniable.

I recommend you drop the name at the beginning of the message ("Hi Stephanie,") or the end ("I hope to hear from you, Stephanie").

▶ No bulky paragraphs

If the first message a new connection sees from you is a giant paragraph, it can end the conversation before it begins.

Keep the paragraphs short (one to two sentences). That way, the writing has a swift pace. Look at how much differently the words below "feel" when written as a long paragraph versus shorter segments.

Long paragraph

"I'm following up from the Chamber of Commerce business roundtable meeting. I remember you said your team needs to find a new janitorial staff for the office. Our company has a 15-year history in the market and already works with a dozen other Chamber members (ex: Acme Corporation, Tech Corporation). Perhaps I could come by to tour the space and give you a quote for our services? Please let me know."

Shorter segments

"I'm following up from the Chamber of Commerce business roundtable meeting. I remember you said your team needs to find a new janitorial staff for the office.

Our company has a 15-year history in the market and already works with a dozen other Chamber members (ex: Acme Corporation, Tech Corporation).

Perhaps I could come by to tour the space and give you a quote for our services?

Please let me know."

———

Think about how each option would hit the eye. Are you more interested in reading option 1 or option 2?

With every LinkedIn networking message, remember:

1. Customization

2. Name-drop

3. No bulky paragraphs

Stay within the three parameters, and every message will have a chance to cut through the noise on LinkedIn and land a response.

Chapter 8
Reports and Presentations

Leave an impression

BEST PRACTICES FOR REPORTS

Raise your hand if you like to read reports.

Anyone?

Anyone?

Few of us like to read a dense summary. That's why the reports **you** compose should be easy to read and perhaps even enjoyable.

How? Follow the checklist below. In Chapter 8, we will walk through examples of effective reports/proposals and uncover ways to hold the reader's attention all the way to the end.

To start, here are the best practices for a leader to demonstrate.

> ▶ **Less is more:** You can't draft a report in a furious writing session, hit "Save" and send it around. Well, you can. But you shouldn't. The editing process is critical. Push yourself to look for sentences or entire sections that are redundant or unnecessary. Ask yourself, "What is the quickest way to make my point?"

▶ **No giant paragraphs:** When readers stumble upon a large chunk of text, they begin to think of one million other tasks they would rather do than read ("Maybe I'll check my Facebook News Feed for the 73rd time today"). Break up the paragraph into smaller sections. The approach is easier on the eyes.

▶ **Be conversational:** Who says a report needs to be written in a buttoned-up, corporate style that feels disconnected to an actual human conversation? Of course, always judge the audience and what people can handle — maybe you can be more casual with an internal team report than a client briefing. But in general, there's no rule that states, "All reports must be dry and painful to read." Still, we do it anyway.

▶ **Stories save the day:** As soon as you begin to share a story, experience or anecdote, the reader will lean in. We love stories, and the technique helps to change the pace — especially if other information in the report is more administrative or procedural. We will go much deeper into storytelling later in the chapter.

BEST PRACTICES FOR PRESENTATIONS

On the previous pages, we talked about best practices for reports so people want to read what you have prepared.

Now, let's turn our focus to presentations (virtual or in person). What can you do so, when you finish, people turn to each other and say, "Excellent presentation right there."

For starters, great speakers and presenters cover the bullet points below.

▶ **Have a plan and execute on it:** Before you step to the mic and utter a word, you need to ask yourself, "What do I plan to say and what is my overall objective?" If the presentation is sales related, you need a clear plan for how to pivot from the product description to a free trial or a way to capture contact information. You cannot figure out a next move on the fly. You will look unprepared. $$$ lost.

- **Eyes on everyone:** The old speaking adage is to "look at the back of the room." That's true because the audience will feel like you see each person. You should also scan the room left to right. Let's say you give a presentation to your board and the room has 16 people in it. As you talk, make eye contact with all 16 people. You will command attention and hold peoples' focus. You look right at them, and they have no choice but to look at you.

- **Don't be the only sound in the room:** When possible, engage the audience. Ask questions, see if people have shared experiences or even have them do a small task or role play. With sales, for example, if someone engages with your product/service (even a teeny, tiny bit), they feel more open to what you sell. Why? They have experienced your "stuff." They have crossed a threshold, and the mood in the room has changed.

- **Always have a story ready:** Step in front of the room with the knowledge that you have at least one great story in your arsenal. And when you deploy the story, you know the crowd will eat it up. Whether the story comes at the beginning, in the middle or as a wrap up (or maybe two stories in different places), a memorable anecdote is a surefire way to keep the eyes on you and drive home your message. We will explore the "raw power" of a story deeper in the chapter.

PROGRESS/STATUS REPORT

If you need to provide a formal status of your work to a client, readability is essential.

For one, you may send the report on behalf of your team. That means the client *and* your employees will judge the document and how well you organized the information.

You also want the progress report to reflect well on your team and the effort everyone has given.

Here's an example of a status report from Acme Corporation, an event planning company. The report goes to the Acme Association, a national membership organization.

Status Report – Acme Corporation Event Planning
November 2019

Team members involved (provide first and last names): person 1, person 2, person 3, etc.

Tasks completed

- Reserved banquet hall and two breakout rooms at Acme Inn and Suites on March 2 and 3 for 2019 Regional Conclave

- Determined menu for breakfast and lunch on both days with the hotel catering staff

- Developed layout for the exhibit hall — <u>see the layout here</u>

- Completed item 4

- Completed item 5, etc.

Tasks for December 2019

- Decide on the dinner menu for the night of March 2 — <u>see the options here</u>

- Order banner to be displayed in the main lobby and signage to direct people to the conference area of the hotel

- Prepare series of emails to encourage early-bird registration by January 15

- Remaining task 4

- Remaining task 5, etc.

Action Items for Acme Association

- Review the dinner options at the link above. What is your top choice?

- What is the early-bird price discount?

▸ Do you want three or four speakers during each breakout session?

▸ Action item 4

▸ Action item 5, etc.

Deeper Insight

The report lays out three areas:

▸ What we (the service provider) did

▸ What we still need to do

▸ What we need you (the client) to do

Sure, you will likely have a conversation about the report and talk through any next steps. The report above frames the discussion and allows the client to see where you need input.

An organized status report is one more way to imply, "We're on the ball and good at what we do."

And the client thinks, "I'm sure glad I hired them."

STRATEGIC PLAN

What good is a new strategy without an organized plan to turn the idea into reality?

As a leader, words are empty without substance to back them up. Even if you hatch a genius new scheme in the flow of a team meeting, it's important to go back to your desk and put the concept on paper.

Why? Two reasons:

1. When you write down the strategy and take a hard look, you might find ways to improve the rough sketch floating in your head.

2. Your team needs a formal outline to reference as the work begins.

A solid strategic plan contains three pieces of information:

1. Objective
2. Strategy
3. Action item(s)

You must explain your overall goal (1), how you will achieve the goal (2) and the tactical steps to reach the goal (3).

The organized approach is useful for all parties. Plus, the simple outline speaks to your detail-oriented approach to leadership.

Here's an example:

Objective: Increase e-commerce sales through the company website by 23% in FY 2020.

Strategy: Develop a broad digital marketing strategy that includes advertising banners/displays and social media content.

Action items:

▸ Hold a planning meeting with the marketing staff to lay out a plan for FY 2020

▸ Research top competitors and understand how they use online advertising (**Lee** will create report)

▸ Design new online banners by December 7 for staff review (**Mark** and **Erika** will work on the designs)

▸ Action item 4

▸ Action item 5

NOTE: The names are in bold so the people don't overlook their responsibilities.

Be descriptive in your strategic plan but each time consider the three phases (Objective, Strategy and Action Items).

Give your team a clear path ahead. It's the best way to start on an ambitious new venture.

EXECUTIVE SUMMARY

An executive summary should be a brief outline of a proposal or longer document.

Why? The summary is written for executives, and people in charge are busy. They *demand* a report that's concise.

Executive summaries matter in all kinds of scenarios. Below, we see an example from a data research firm as the company's president shares findings with the client.

Clients will breathe a sigh of relief when they see your report is contained to one page.

Less. Is. More.

———

First paragraph: spell out the main findings

Give the reader a top-line summary. For instance:

In the report that follows, we examine audience engagement while people use two or more devices at one time (ex: cell phone and television). The study took place in 8,273 U.S. households between the dates of September and November 2018.

The main finding: as the number of devices increased, the person's social media conversations increased too — sometimes by as much as 74%.

Second paragraph: summary of the details inside the report

Then, provide additional information to back up the top-line summary.

In the case of the example here (audience engagement), the second paragraph could include an overview of how the team gathered data and more about the demographics of the people monitored.

Third paragraph: draw conclusions

Share final thoughts about the report and broad takeaways executives could glean if they only read a one-page synopsis.

———

Your ultimate goal is to allow an executive to read the summary in a few minutes, walk into a meeting and look brilliant with the insights you shared.

Short. Sweet. Smart.

That's an executive summary in a nutshell.

The raw power of a great story

OVERVIEW

Have a big presentation or report on the horizon?

Stop right there. Before you make one click or drag in your PowerPoint or Prezi, ask yourself a question:

- What story or stories can I share to reinforce the value of my product or service?

Numbers and data are critical, yes. And your talk should incorporate all relevant statistics that make your business shine.

But a story breathes life into the data and makes a human connection with the audience.

The story can come in a variety of forms, but here are my two favorites:

1. How your company came to be

2. How your product or service made a difference in someone's life

People often want to know, "How did you get into this business?"

The answer: a short recap of your journey from day one until now.

And after the sales pitch, reinforce your claims with an honest-to-goodness example of past performance.

Great data and a killer story — who can stop you now?

In the following pages, we explore how to integrate storytelling into several classic presentation or report scenarios.

- Sales deck/sales presentation
- Sales proposal
- Training manual/training session
- Grant application
- Annual report

You have worked hard to gain the customer success examples. Now it's time to put the stories to work.

Let's tell some stories.

SALES DECK/SALES PRESENTATION

Where does storytelling fit into a sales deck or sales presentation?

In my opinion, you can catch the reader's attention in one of two places:

1. At the beginning (the first words you write or say to a crowd)

2. In the middle (after you describe the product/service)

Either way, a story "wakes up" the audience and adds a human layer to your offer. Plus, the colorful description allows the audience to see how the product/service could benefit them too.

Let's start with tactic #1 and kick off the sales pitch with a story. The product/service description comes second.

Imagine the person opens your email attachment and views your sales presentation for the first time. "Let's see what they got," the person thinks.

Or the person looks up from his/her cell phone and sees you approach the mic.

In either case, boom! A story front and center. Here's an example:

———

First section: Lay out the problem you faced

Every fall, I would feel the chill in the air and see the leaves begin to sway in the trees. I would think: Oh no, here they come.

Note: Do you think the audience is paying attention now? You better believe it.

Second section: Expand on the intrigue you created in the first section.

As a native New Englander, I know raking leaves is a fact of life. But year after year, the task became tougher and tougher on my back. It seems like we've done the work the same way for generations — rake the leaves into piles and move them into yard bags.

There had to be a better way.

Note: OK you've identified the pain point (literally, too, with the back discomfort). Now fix the issue.

Third section: Explain the solution to the problem

In the fall of 2018, I decided to experiment. I purchased thin netting material and measured the width and length of my yard.

I laid the netting across the lawn — it was so lightweight and see-through you could barely notice it. Then, I watched the leaves start to fall.

Note: The audience thinks, "OK so what happened in the end?" Suspense is a wonderful sales tool.

Fourth section: What was the outcome?

Once the leaves blanketed the yard, my son and I grabbed the corners of the netting and voila — we "raked up" all the leaves in a matter of minutes.

Note: "A-ha" moment for the audience. The big payoff. Also imagine the audience sees photos or videos of the product at work.

Fifth section: Closing line

That day, Acme Net Raker was born.

Then, launch into a typical intro.

Hi, my name is Ron Derry, and I am the creator of Acme Net Raker. Today, my team of 22 people manufacture and sell our product in 700 stores in the New England area and…

[continues with info on the product and sales figures]

Deeper Insight

The story pulls the reader in and *then* we learn basic details like the person's name and sales figures.

Could you flip the two sections and start with the basic intro? Sure.

I am partial to the story in the first position because it will hook the audience and connect with people on an emotional level.

No one likes raking leaves! We can all relate to the frustration in the story.

Now think about the product(s) or service(s) you provide. What kind of story can you share to kick off a sales deck or sales presentation?

A few ideas:

▶ The "origin story" of how your company came to be

▶ Memorable client success after the person used your product/service

▶ Example of someone who, at first, didn't believe your product/service would work but is now a true believer

Draw upon the success stories you "own." There's no better place than a sales pitch to place the examples front and center.

TRAINING MANUAL/TRAINING SESSION

As a leader you always want to look for opportunities to defy expectations.

Employees hear the words "training session," and they already start to imagine how drab the day will be.

Not so fast. With a mix of storytelling and role playing, you can make a training session hands-on and lively. Or if you need to draft a 25-page training guide, infuse the writing with stories to keep the reader moving down the page.

Here are two ways to infuse stories:

1. Use stories to show examples of rules and regulations

As often as possible, share with the group a real or fictitious situation related to a particular aspect of the training.

Example from a sales training manual:

With sales "cold calls," always end the discussion with a next step in the process.

Read the story below to understand why.

January 2018: CEO Jerry McDougal (that's me) had a great kick-off phone call with a solid new lead. I told the lead I would send product samples and the person responded with, "Thanks. Our team will take a look and get back to you in a few weeks."

Innocently, I responded with, "Sure. Take your time. I will reach back out over email and see what you think."

Guess what? I sent three follow-up emails and called the person's desk at least 12 times. He never answered, and we have not yet spoken again.

February 2018: I had another quality initial conversation with a lead. This time, I took a new approach. At the end of the call, I asked the person, "When is the best time for us to speak again to gain your thoughts on the product? I will send you an invitation for the call."

Two weeks later, I called at the scheduled time and the conversation continued without a hitch. The person is now one of our top customers.

Lesson learned — always have a next step in mind during sales calls.

2. Incorporate role playing to drive home new ideas

Example from a sales training session:

How should we react when the sales lead says over the phone, "I'm busy. Can you just email me information, and I can review that way?"

Classic brush-off move, right? Practice as a team how to fight through and keep the person on the phone.

As an example, the team could break into pairs and one person will be the skeptical potential customer. Your job is to condense your pitch into 30 seconds and put all the information across before the person has a chance to hang up.

When you are playing the role of the customer, be tough! Make the sales rep work hard for the business.

———

To recap: draw upon stories to make training manuals more interesting and understandable. Once people have an example to reference, the rule becomes clearer to follow.

And with training sessions, the best way to learn is to "get your hands dirty." Through role playing, the lessons will stick, and the time will pass much faster. In fact, people might not even check the clock — they're too busy to be bored.

SALES PROPOSAL

Stories are a dynamic way to round out a sales proposal.

Yes, it's nice to include a client headshot + testimonial and to list off current clients. Both tactics validate other people have hired you.

But a short anecdote of past success adds color and personality to your pitch.

I believe the best place for a story is after you lay out the work you plan to do and the pricing. Right when the person thinks, "Is this company worth the cost?"... BAM, hit 'em with a story.

The company in the example below, Acme IT, provides IT services. Imagine the potential customer reads the company's pricing, turns the page and then finds the following.

The Day the Screens Went Dark

October 2, 2018 at 9:34 a.m. My cell phone rings. It's a long-time client who has depended on Acme IT services for his company of 34 employees.

His voice was in a panic. "All 41 of our computer screens went black! What do we do?"

Right away, I dispatched three of our Acme technicians to visit the client's office and troubleshoot the problem.

Within an hour, we found the issue. An employee had clicked on a link in an email that contained a virus. The infected computer then spread across the office and caused all screens in the network to go dark.

Our team eliminated the virus, reset the network and the computers returned to life.

The client was relieved, and the work could resume.

For Acme IT, it was another chance to prove we are there for our clients no matter what.

———

A few points about the story:

- The story is quick. The potential client did not turn the pricing page over to find 2,000 words.

- If you can mention the client by name, that's great. If you can't because of privacy concerns or other reasons, you should still consider the story. Don't waste examples of how you achieve results.

- Note the use of numbers — another subtle element that enhances the story.
    - 9:34 a.m.
    - 34 employees

- ○ 41 computers
- ○ within an hour

Take the reader inside the situation. Use available numbers to heighten the drama. **Make the reader feel something.**

▸ You don't need to be a "writer." You are not auditioning to pen spy thrillers. You are leveraging a past success to drive the next one. Discuss with your team the most relevant story to share with a potential client. Which example(s) will resonate the most?

▸ Lastly, incorporate visuals when available to enrich the story. Do you have photos, videos or tables? Don't go nuts and include 17 pie charts — you need to keep the story moving. But a visual or two will make the story even more compelling.

GRANT APPLICATIONS AND ANNUAL REPORTS

In the non-profit world, storytelling should find its way into two classic writing scenarios: grant applications and annual reports.

Why? When you ask for money — from either a grant-making organization or donors — you need to share a real, human moment that describes the impact you make.

In *Wait, How Do I Promote My Business?*, my book on writing to spread the word about your company/organization, I share an entire template for a story in a grant application (the story can also double as a feature in an annual report).

I will not lay out the exact same template here. Rather, I will share best practices so your story will tug on the heartstrings and bring in the dollars.

▸ **Take the reader inside someone's life**
  ○ Don't stay at the surface level and explain how you help "many people." Pick one person who represents your mission and share that person's journey (with permission, of course).

► **Include a beginning, middle and end**
   o Beginning: Explain how the profile person struggled until your organization came to the rescue.
   o Middle: List action items your organization completed to better the person's situation (steps 1, 2, 3 and so on).
   o End: Share how the person has improved thanks to your efforts.

► **Mine the story for tiny details**
   o If the person came to you hungry, how much did he weigh? Don't write, "He was skinny." Go with, "He was 16 years old but only 87 pounds." Do you *feel* the difference? Readers will.
   o Find numbers that add dimension to the story and run with them.

► **Include a photo of the profiled person**
   o If a photo exists and you can use it, do so. Otherwise, readers have to imagine the person you helped. If readers can see the person firsthand, they will feel even more connected to the situation.

► **Think small**
   o It's OK to focus on one person as a representative of the whole. Readers have trouble staying focused when all they can see is a view from 30,000 feet.
   o Take the audience down to the ground level and make them stare straight at someone else's struggle. Prove you can better a person's life, and you stand a great chance at new funding.

Chapter 9
Lead by Action

Personal accountability

THE #1 QUALITY YOU NEED TO POSSESS EVERY DAY

Let me start chapter 9 with the main point front and center.

If you're not willing to **follow up** (the #1 quality) as a leader every single day (no exceptions), then you won't find success. It's impossible.

See, following up is the secret ingredient that drives projects forward and ensures you will, in time, realize your goals.

By the same token, following up is the most grueling, painstaking and demanding aspect of building something special. When you wake up in the morning, it's right there at the top of the to-do list. It never goes away.

With any new business or initiative, the outside world is skeptical. People are content with the product or service they already have; why should they care what *you* offer? You couldn't possibly make the situation any better, right? Or so they think.

That's why, like clockwork, potential customers ignore your emails, screen your phone calls and generally keep their distance. Over. And over. And over.

Leave me alone, they say without saying. *I'm not interested.*

Then, you have two choices. Walk away or follow up.

If you stop trying, the project stalls. And your team loses. Game over.

You're another headstone in the cemetery of failed businesses because you weren't willing to stay in the fight.

The need to try, try and try again is as germane to business as paying taxes. *It's part of the game, and there's no escape.*

That's why, down below, I have included templates for three common follow-up scenarios in business. As a leader, I hope you will find opportunities to use the guides.

1. How to follow up if someone ignores your first email

Reply to the previous email you sent:

Hi _____,

I'm following up to make sure you saw the email I sent [earlier this week/ late last week] about [quick info about the issue at hand; for instance, "the Collins proposal"].

Please let me know.

Thanks again,

– Leader's first name

Deeper insight: The message is short and sweet. Plus, you remind the person what the email is about (ex: "Collins proposal").

2. How to follow up if someone promised to do a favor/task but never did

Reply to the previous email you sent:

Hi _____,

I'm following up to make sure you're still able to [the favor/task; for instance, "introduce me to Gloria Rodriguez via email"].

Please let me know if that's possible.

Thanks so much,

– Leader's first name

Deeper insight: Again, details matter with the follow-up message. Gently remind the person what he/she promised to do (ex: intro to Gloria Rodriguez). When people offer to open a big door for you, *don't let them off the hook.*

3. How to follow up when it's clear the person is avoiding you

OK, it feels an awful lot like the person doesn't want to deal with you. I get it — no fun following up.

But again, you have no choice but to keep trying because your project depends on a response.

Hi _____,

I know you've received several messages from me, but I would still appreciate if you could [whatever you need the person to do; for instance, "take a look at the first draft of my short story and give me your honest feedback"].

[Then, explain in one line why you would appreciate the help; for instance, "You have a keen eye, and I know you can take my work from good to great."]

Thanks again for the help,

– Leader's first name

Deeper insight: First, speak to the fact that you already sent "several messages." Put it out there and move on. Then, remind the person what you need and explain why you respect his/her opinion.

———

OK, huddle up. If you care about the work, then you have no choice but to follow up with all your heart and soul.

Eat, drink, follow up, sleep, repeat. That's who you are as a leader.

And if emails won't do the trick, pick up the phone and stay in pursuit.

SAY GOODBYE TO "I DON'T DISAGREE"

I have yet to drop the words "pet peeve," but I can't hold back when I discuss the next topic.

Here it goes: I groan when I hear people (leaders or otherwise) use the phrase, "I don't disagree."

What people mean is, "I am not willing to admit you are correct. I will instead say I am not opposed to what you have to say."

Yuck. Why is it so hard to tell people they're right? Does it make you, in turn, wrong to give someone else validation and a little time in the sun?

No! Not even a little bit. In fact, the move makes others feel valued.

And especially for leaders — yes, you are allowed to let other people look smart. You will gain someone's trust and show you are comfortable giving people credit.

From now on, toss "I don't disagree" into the dustbin of worn-out expressions.

"I agree with you."

Let someone be right. It will be OK.

#rantover #stillpeeved

AVOID THE ROYAL "YOU"

How many times in an interview — particularly with athletes — have you heard the following line?

"Yes, today was a big win. You try so hard all season and you give it your best on the field, and you just have to appreciate what it takes to compete at this level."

OK, a question. Who is "you" in this case? Who is the athlete talking about?

When we talk, why do we so often use the second person? Obviously, the athlete in my example refers to himself or herself when saying, "You try so hard all season." So why the royal "You"?

Here's my assessment: When we are asked to talk about ourselves, we feel funny using "I" because it seems like bragging or speaking out of turn.

"I try so hard all season, and I give it my best on the field."

Instead, we insert a "you" to deflect attention or praise.

But the "you" is incorrect and a passive way to discuss our efforts.

As a leader, you may conduct interviews with media or speak to team members/ clients. When those moments arise, catch yourself dropping "you" and instead opt for "I" and "we."

Here's an example of the wrong way:

"When **you** land a big client, **your** next move is to make sure **you** are prepared for the challenges ahead. As a team leader, **you** never know when issues will arise, but **you** need to be ready."

Bleh. All the "you" and "your" are impersonal.

Let's try again:

"When **we** land a big client, our next move is to make sure **we** are prepared for the challenges ahead. As a team leader, **I** never know when issues will arise, but **I** need to be ready."

Now the quote feels like it comes from the speaker directly. The tone is more assertive and confident, right?

We replace "I" with "you" so much in our day-to-day conversations that the mistake often filters into our writing and public speaking.

Keep a close watch on "you." When it happens, take a pause and then switch to "I." You may also want to use "we" when you incorporate the efforts of your team members (a topic we discuss on page 6).

The best leaders speak with authenticity and from the heart.

A steady dose of "I" will get you there.

UNDERPROMISE AND OVERDELIVER

"Say a little and do a lot."

"Let your actions speak for themselves."

"Show me. Don't tell me."

The maxims about hard work can go on for days. It's easy to copy/paste one of the timeless expressions and create a flashy meme.

But what do the quotes mean in the context of leading your team? **What does work ethic look like in real life?**

In this book, we're all about the practical side of leadership and the nitty gritty moments when you need to "let your actions speak for themselves."

Less theory, more doing.

Here are three examples.

1. You wrap up a staff discussion about how to sell a new product. You can tell the team still has a rough idea about the product and the best ways to offer the item to new and existing customers.

That night, you spend an hour and draft a sales manual for the new product. You share best practices for email/phone engagements and a follow-up process with interested buyers.

The next day, you email the team the finished sales manual as a shared document. You didn't make a big deal that you were "going to stay up all night and work on the manual." In fact, you didn't tell anyone at all.

No, you went home, sat at the computer and knocked it out.

Then, when the team sees the manual in the morning, it comes as a welcomed surprise.

You saw a need. You worked hard to *meet* the need. Nothing more to it.

In other words, "Say a little and do a lot."

2. You want to give your development staff a leg up during next year's fundraising push.

You look across your network and find an outside expert on capital campaigns and fundraising drives. You coordinate for the person to lead a half-day workshop for the development team.

You're the leader so the decision to coordinate the workshop rests in your hands. You don't delegate out the decision or talk about bringing in an expert — and then never follow through on the idea.

No. You do research, make phone calls, schedule the workshop and make it happen.

In other words, you "let your actions speak for themselves."

3. You have a policy that all nine employees can attend one professional development conference or event per year on the company's dime.

You realize such an offer, while generous, can overwhelm staff members who may not be familiar with the conference circuit.

That's when you step into action. Without broadcasting your plans, you spend an afternoon and identify two or three appropriate conferences for each employee.

You then send an email to every employee, share the conference options and ask people to choose one (or to share another conference they found on their own).

Did employees ask you to research the conferences? No. Is it helpful that you put in the time anyway? Yes.

You didn't need to make a big pronouncement like, "No calls on Tuesday afternoon. I will spend the time researching conferences for everyone."

No. You did the work. Plain and simple. And now your employees can make plans to attend conferences that will sharpen their skills and, ideally, boost your bottom line.

In other words, "Show me. Don't tell me."

———

Leadership is a collection of all the little moments where you decide to make stuff happen, set new ideas in motion and put your employees in a position to be successful.

Anyone can make a motivational poster.

But it takes a special person to **lead**.

WHEN YOUR PRAISE STARTS TO SOUND THE SAME

"Great work, Tim"

"Excellent stuff, Gina"

"Well done, everyone"

Isn't it enough to give someone a basic compliment? Sometimes, yes.

All the time? No.

As I discuss throughout the book, employees scrutinize a leader's words every day. You're in charge, and employees hold you to a higher standard — even when you dish out praise.

"The only thing I ever hear Greg say when he's trying to be nice is 'Well done.' Does he even mean it?"

Good news. There's a simple way to break up the monotony: take your compliment one step further whether it's over email, on the phone or in person.

- ▶ *"Great work, Tim. The front cover design of the new catalog looks sleek. Customers will love it."*

- ▶ *"Excellent stuff, Gina. Your presentation held the client's attention for all 20 minutes. That's not easy to do."*

- ▶ *"Well done, everyone. The initial engagement meeting with the new client went perfectly, and I already received a positive note from Jack McFarland, the CEO, about being excited to work with us."*

It's a simple formula. Offer a compliment ("Great work, Tim.") and then include a more specific reason for the kind words.

It's nice to know you liked someone's effort but extra meaningful when you explain WHY you appreciate it.

Practice the approach with compliments and watch the reaction.

Group dynamics

HOW TO LEAD A MEETING — BRIEF BUT RELEVANT

In every business, there's perhaps no more dreaded word than...

Meeting.

No one likes to sit in meetings. They tend to break up the flow of the day or hold people hostage from other tasks.

Of course, sometimes meetings are necessary. When it *is* time to bring your team around the table, keep in mind two main points so the meeting is brief yet productive.

1. Map out the discussion ahead of time

2. Know when to let the conversation percolate and when to shut it down

Point 1 is well understood. Plan ahead and think through the conversation.

Point 2 is more nuanced. As a leader, you should foster dialogue on an important issue, but you also can't sit in the room forever. Where's the balance?

Let's explore both points.

Map out the discussion ahead of time

The meeting's printed (or posted) agenda is critical as the document sets forth what everyone will discuss and in what order.

You should consider lighter pieces of business at the front of the meeting to set aside extra time for a heavier topic that warrants discussion.

FOR EXAMPLE:

MEETING AGENDA
[Name of Organization]
[Month/Day/Year; for instance, "December 17, 2019"]

– Review of last meeting's notes

– Updates on roles and responsibilities

– Extension on Robertson proposal deadline

– Discussion: Entering the robotics industry

If you know, for example, the conversation around robotics will take time, then clear out other business.

Know when to let the conversation percolate and when to shut it down

Dialogue around an agenda item — or a topic not on the agenda — can happen at any time.

And that's a positive. You want your team engaged on an issue that could impact the future of the business.

Your role as the leader may also be to serve as a facilitator. Sit back, listen to your team and decide if you should keep the chatter going.

Ask yourself:

- Is the discussion helpful to the overall growth of the business? If yes, let people talk and see what ideas emerge.

- Is the discussion too narrow in scope and perhaps relevant to a select number of people on the team? If yes, consider cutting in with, "Can the people on this particular project hold a separate conversation after this meeting so we keep everything moving?"

Leaders always need to judge the merits of a longer conversation in a staff meeting. It's possible someone utters a brilliant idea seven minutes into a drawn-out discussion. If you ended the dialogue at four minutes, the smart insight may have never emerged.

Even if the meeting goes a bit longer than employees hoped, you showed you did all you could to respect everyone's time. And the team will appreciate your mindfulness.

DELEGATE LIKE THERE'S NO TOMORROW

With every new task, leaders face a classic challenge:

Do I complete the work myself or delegate to someone else?

Yes, there are times when it's best to handle the load on your own. Just. Get. It. Done.

Then again, there are other moments when it's best to take the work off your plate and, at the same time, empower other people on your team.

To delegate or not to delegate? As a leader, that **is** the central question. Day after day after day.

First, here are the merits of delegation.

- **Make your life easier** — Even though you're in charge, you can't do everything yourself. In fact, your company/organization *won't* run well if you do try to handle all the work.

- **Your employees can't grow unless they are given challenges** — Professional development is more than a series of workshops *about* professional development. Your people need real-life challenges. Let them step up.

- **Delegation = buy in** — Let's say you founded the company. You might be the most passionate person about the work that goes on because, well, this is all your idea. When you delegate tasks, you draw employees closer to the work and the impact behind it.

- **Show you can trust others** — You hired these people or at least manage them. Prove you believe in their ability to oversee a challenge or opportunity.

Below is an email template if you want to delegate to one person.

Subject line: Need your help with [project at hand; for instance, "the Fleming account"]

Hi [employee's first name],

[Set up the situation; for instance, "It looks like we're a go with the Fleming account, and they have already asked for a kick-off meeting next Wednesday at 3 p.m. in their offices."]

[Then, the delegation; for instance, "I would like you to take over the account as the lead project manager."]

[Then, explain why you chose the particular employee; for instance, "I saw the work you did in a support role with the Anderson account, and I think you're ready to manage a client on your own. You proved you could juggle several tasks and a client who needs constant communication."]

[Then, the next step; for instance, "Drop by my office before the end of the day so I can give you a few more tips about the account and answer any questions."]

Thanks,

– Leader's first name

Email signature

Deeper Insight

The subject line cuts right to the heart of the matter ("Need your help…") so the employee knows what's going on.

Then, it's important to explain *why* you have chosen to delegate the work ("you proved you could juggle several tasks"). That language gives the employee added confidence and the belief that he/she is rewarded with greater responsibility.

In one message, you lighten your load and embolden someone on your team. That's an efficient email.

FIND THE PERSON IN THE CORNER

Leaders are aware of every person in the room.

They keep their eyes open and see opportunities to build connections and bring people into the fold.

Here's a scenario:

Your team goes to a baseball game as an office outing. Before the game, everyone eats hot dogs and socializes in a picnic area. Many employees came with spouses and their kids.

152

One of your new employees, Tim, is single and at the game by himself. You notice he's sitting on the end of the picnic table staring at his phone — likely because he doesn't know many co-workers yet.

As a team leader, you walk over and see how Tim's doing. Then you ask if he's met two folks on your team who work in another division. You walk Tim over to those two people and make introductions.

The three people engage in conversation. You politely step out of the mix to scan the picnic area again and see who else might now be "in the corner."

Deeper Insight

Too often, "leadership development" centers on how leaders react in times of crisis or great challenge.

What about those non-descript moments you could easily miss if you don't pay attention?

People who sit "in the corner" are a classic example. Your job as a leader is to **lead.** That means, in part, to make sure all people are accounted for and included.

LET EVERYONE HAVE A SAY

Leaders need to have eyes and ears in the back of their heads...and the left side... and the right side too.

That's because, when you lead a group discussion or other team-building exercise, you must be aware of each person's level of engagement.

More to the point, it's important you hear from everyone in the room.

Since you're the leader and in charge of the situation, it's your responsibility to keep tabs on each person. It's unlikely someone else within the group will stop and say, "I don't think Phil has spoken much so far. Phil, what do you think?"

No. It's **your** job to bring Phil into the discussion. Otherwise, the moment will come and go, Phil won't talk and everyone will disperse none the wiser.

Here are a few strategies to make certain the "Phils" of the world always have a say.

▶ **Listen with your ears *and* your eyes**

O. As the discussion or event unfolds, keep watch on everyone and make a mental tally of who has spoken and who remains silent.

▶ **Don't be afraid to call someone out**

O Would some people rather slink into the chair and never participate? Of course. But you're the leader, and you want everyone to contribute.

O "Celia, we haven't heard from you yet. Any thoughts on the conversation?" Even if Celia would prefer to keep quiet, you did your best to bring her into the fold and value what she has to say.

▶ **Don't be afraid to shut somebody up**

O On the other end of the spectrum, you may have people who contribute *too* much. As a leader, it's appropriate to say, "Thanks for all of your thoughts, Michael. Let's hear from a few other people who haven't shared any opinions yet."

▶ **Sometimes, people need a nudge**

O Often, employees (and clients) only "speak when spoken to," as the expression goes. But if you call upon them, you might unlock something special and add a meaningful voice to the room. The only way to find out is to give a little push.

▶ **Same goes for conference calls and video chats**

O Whether everyone is in the same room or dialing in from three different continents, the rules of leadership apply. Allow each person a chance to speak or at least let people know you want their opinions.

Chapter 10

Write as a Leader in a Student Organization

First, create an email signature

Before you can send emails on behalf of a student (or membership) organization, you need an email signature.

The signature appears at the end of your emails and includes relevant bio and contact information.

Let's go over the basics of an email signature for a student at any grade level or in college.

YOUR NAME

TITLE, STUDENT ORGANIZATION

NAME OF SCHOOL, CLASS OF _____

EMAIL | CELL: XXX-XXX-XXXX

JOSH DOVER

TREASURER, STUDENT GOVERNMENT ASSOCIATION

ACME HIGH SCHOOL, CLASS OF 2021

JOSH@ACMEHIGH.EDU | CELL: 555-555-5555

Deeper Insight

The email signature allows Josh to explain his title, name of the organization, name of the school and graduation year.

He also includes an email address and cell phone. It's up to you (or perhaps your school) if you're allowed to share a phone number.

Have your email signature ready? OK, now we can learn to write common student leadership emails.

Event planning

HOW TO WRITE A PLAN FOR A NEW PROJECT

If you have an idea for a new initiative, you must be organized and make a strong case. Why? You might need the approval of administrators, teachers or classmates.

Follow the outline below to ensure your proposal addresses all the important areas.

Proposal: Electronics Disposal Day at Acme High School

Section 1: Overview

Here, explain the project and why it matters. Make the case right away.

In our school and the broader community, we have many electronic items (ex: computers, tablets) that people no longer use. We need to dispose of the devices properly so they don't harm the environment.

> The Acme High School Student Association proposes a day-long event in which people can safely discard their unused devices at a central location.

Section 2: Why our project matters

Next, use hard evidence (ex: statistics) to help the reader understand the scope of the problem you want to solve. Numbers prove your point like nothing else.

EXAMPLE:

> The Acme High School Student Association programs committee spoke with Mr. Berringer, the IT director at Acme High School, and learned our school has 72 older, unused laptops the school needs to discard.
>
> > NOTE: Read the last few words again — "unused laptops the school needs to discard." The school is the subject so the line is in active voice. It's more assertive than, "unused laptops that need to be discarded by the school."
>
> We also did a poll of our group's 51 members and found we collectively have 287 devices we no longer need.
>
> That's over 300 devices between the school and our membership. We feel there are hundreds of similar, unwanted devices in our school community.

Section 3: Implementation plan

Share the logistics required to make the project happen.

EXAMPLE:

> We propose to hold our event on Saturday, April 17 from 8 a.m. to 3 p.m. in the school parking lot adjacent to the gym.
>
> People can bring their devices for proper disposal.
>
> We also want to have face painting for kids, a popcorn machine and a DJ who plays music.

Section 4: Costs

Take your time with section 4 and have a solid grasp on expenses. You can't run with your idea until you know what it will cost.

EXAMPLE:

> We can partner with Acme Electronics Disposal. The company will charge us $350 to set up in the parking lot.
> Face-painting: free
> Use of school's popcorn machine: $50
> DJ: $100

Section 5: The team behind the project

Explain who will work on the initiative so decision makers have the confidence to give an approval.

EXAMPLE:

> We have developed an Electronics Disposal Day committee.
> Committee Chair: [First and last name]
> Committee members: [List all first and last names]

Section 6: Next steps

Now that you laid out your plan, where do you go from here?

EXAMPLE:

> Thank you for reviewing our proposal. Please let us know if you have questions or concerns.
>
> As we are already into March, we would like to begin planning as soon as possible. We hope you can make a decision soon.

Thanks,

– Student's first and last name

Chair, Electronics Disposal Day committee

Deeper Insight

The proposal covers the classic questions: who, what, when, where, why and how.

If you address all six, the reader (ex: your school's administrators) will have all the information they need to decide.

Plus, the proposal shows you already thought hard about logistics, costs and why the project is important to the community.

HOW TO REQUEST KEYNOTE SPEAKERS OR WORKSHOP PRESENTERS

As you plan a conference or event, you may need to invite people to be keynote speakers or workshop presenters.

Your outreach must be polite, brief and authentic so the person is encouraged to reply and participate in your program.

Here's how:

Subject line: Interest in being a [what you want the person to do; for instance, "keynote speaker" or "workshop presenter"] for [name of event]

Hi [Mr./Ms. _____],

My name is [first and last name], and I am a/an/the [leadership title] with [name of student organization]. We are [short description of your group; for instance, "the leading student organization in the U.S. for jobs in farming and agriculture"].

I'm writing to [the nature of your message; for instance, "invite you to be a keynote speaker at our Rise Up National Conference over the weekend of October 5–7 in Kansas City, Missouri"].

[Then, provide at least one reason why you chose to ask the person to be part of the event and be specific; for instance, "I spent time on your website and enjoyed your blog, especially your post about entrepreneurship tips for people in the farming industry. Your advice about becoming an expert in a specialty or niche stuck with me."]

> NOTE: The previous section is strategic. It's not enough to tell the person, "I think you're great!" Give a clear example, prove you did your homework and link to the person's achievements to show you spent time in his/her world.

[Finally, include any details the person needs to know right now as he/she assesses the opportunity; for instance, "We still have openings for keynote speakers on October 6 and October 7. You would present for 90 minutes before a crowd of 2,500 students and teachers."]

Here's more information on the [name of the event; for instance, "Rise Up National Conference"].

Please let me know your level of interest. I am happy to discuss logistics like travel and cost.

Thanks,

– Leader's first and last name

Email signature

Deeper Insight

The email is courteous, informative and genuine all at once. Also, wherever you see underlined text is an example of a hyperlink.

While the person will be honored you reached out in the first place, your pitch is extra impressive when you demonstrate you did your homework (ex: "I spent time on your website…").

And if the person is an in-demand speaker, your request needs to be a cut above the competition. That's why a special reference to the person's work or recent accomplishment is the smart way to go.

The approach is gratifying to the speaker and helps you build trust even before you talk or meet in person.

HOW TO COMMUNICATE WITH TEACHERS ABOUT AN UPCOMING EVENT

When you need students to sign up and attend your conference or event, teachers are your best ambassadors and sharers.

Teachers need to easily process the event information and pass the message onto students (and their parents).

The email template here will help you achieve both ends.

Subject line: Spreading the word with your students about [name of conference or event]

Hi [Mr./Ms. ____],

My name is [first and last name], and I am a/an/the [leadership title] with [name of student organization]. We are [short description of your group; for instance, "the leading student organization in the U.S. for jobs in farming and agriculture"].

I'm writing to [the nature of your message; for instance, "invite your students to attend our Rise Up National Conference over the weekend of October 5–7 in Kansas City, Missouri"].

[Then, provide three bullet points on why students should come; for instance:

- "Our keynote speaker is Kim Johnson from the hit TV show, 'House Builders.'

- We expect more than 2,500 students to attend so it's a perfect place to meet other teens interested in careers in agriculture.

- We have awesome excursions planned like a day trip to the Acme Water Park."]

NOTE: Be specific in your bullet points. Name drop important people like keynote speakers and give an example of conference highlights (ex: Acme Water Park).

[Finally, give all pertinent links and explain next steps. For instance:

"Here are the links your students need:

- Registration for Rise Up National Conference

- Hotel and travel information

- Cost information

- Program schedule and speaker bios"]

Can you please let me know you received my email?

Thanks, and I hope you and your students can attend!

– Leader's first and last name

Email signature

Deeper Insight

First, make sure you introduce yourself, share your job title and give a bit of explanation about your student group. Never assume the reader knows who you are and what you do.

Even if you're 100% certain the teacher *does* recognize your group, what if he/she forwards the message to someone else? The new person may need to start with the basics. Always over-communicate!

Share highlights of the event in bullet points so the person can process each item. And include all relevant links so the teacher doesn't need to write back with, "Thanks! Can you send me travel information?"

Lastly, make particular note of the sentence that reads:

Can you please let me know you received my email?

The line is a strategy often used by salespeople. Ask the person to confirm receipt of your message.

For one, you will know if the email came through OK. As well, you encourage the person to "act" on your email.

If you don't receive an answer after 48 hours, reply back to your original email with:

"Hi there,

Please let me know you saw my email from earlier in the week about the Rise Up National Conference.

Thanks again!"

Even though you're a student and the teacher is an adult, you have every right to push for a response. That kind of polite persistence is a terrific quality in any leader.

HOW TO ASK ANOTHER STUDENT GROUP TO CO-SPONSOR AN EVENT

When you want to partner with another organization — student or otherwise — to host an event, your email must be direct and explain your objectives.

That way, your email becomes a starting point for a deeper conversation on how to work together.

In the following email, a leader from the Fashion Club at Acme High School wants to team up with the Photography Club from East High School for an upcoming fashion show.

Subject line: Partnering with [name of your student organization] for [name of your event]

Hi [student leader's first name],

My name is [first and last name], and I am a/an/the [leadership title] with [name of student organization]. We are [short description of your group; for instance, "a 30-person group that learns about fashion trends and hosts two fashion shows per year"].

> NOTE: First, you explain the purpose of your student organization. Next, tell the person what you want to accomplish.

I'm writing to [the nature of your message; for instance, "see if the Photography Club at East High School wants to be the official photography team for our Spring Fashion Show."]

[Then, provide relevant details the person might ask like date, time and event specifics. For instance:

- "The Spring Fashion Show will happen on Friday, March 9 at 7 p.m. in the Acme High auditorium.

- Last spring, we had more than 300 people attend! Here are a few photos.

- We will have 13 'models' showing off our designs.

- This spring, the theme is 'Sustainability' so our designs will feature a lot of repurposed or second-hand clothes."]

NOTE: See how the bulleted list also contains a link to photos from a previous event. When possible, give the student leader visual proof your event is substantial and worth joining.

Again, please let me know if the Photography Club would like to partner with us.

Thanks, and I hope to hear from you!

– Leader's first and last name

Email signature

Deeper Insight

Notice how the purpose of the message appears in the email subject line and the top of the email right after the introduction.

Provide relevant facts about your event and then ask the person to again tell you if he/she wants to collaborate or work together.

If you don't receive an answer after 48 hours, reply to your original email with:

"Hi [person's first name],

Please let me know you saw my previous message about the fashion show.

Thanks again!"

Marketing and public relations

HOW TO PITCH YOUR STUDENT GROUP TO POTENTIAL MEMBERS

As a student leader, you might need to recruit new members. Those potential members could come from middle school, high school or even college.

No matter the audience, there's one strategy for recruitment that works better than all the others.

Tell a story.

When you first walk in the room, the crowd is skeptical.

"Why should I join your group?" everyone thinks. "What's so special about it?"

You need to win people over and make them understand your student organization is worthwhile. The best way is to share an example of how the group has made an impact on you.

It's not enough to tell the room how your group is "amazing" and "really fun." Plan out a story you want to tell, and you will have everyone's full attention. People of any age love a good story.

EXAMPLE:

Hi, everybody. Thanks for letting me stop by your classroom and explain to you why I love being in the Acme Student Association or "ASA."

This is my third year in the organization, and now I am vice president of membership.

The ASA helps to plan many of our school's biggest events like homecoming and prom. We also host fundraisers and help with school spirit activities throughout the year.

I could stand here and tell you ASA is awesome, but I'd rather share a quick story about what we do and how we make a difference at Acme High.

Last fall, the ASA had the chance to design the chalk inside the end-zones on the football field. Usually, the end-zones have the words "Go Bears." Principal Walker thought it would be cool if we did something more creative. She asked the ASA to coordinate the project.

So, here's what we did: First, we worked as a team to design the end-zones on the computer. We wanted each end-zone to look differently but also stress the importance of diversity and inclusion.

Then we went to the football field with Mr. Hooper, the computer science teacher, and used the school's drone to map out the size of our design. We all got to use the drone and fly it around!

We shared our design with the school's maintenance crew and helped them turn our idea in reality.

At the big game against East High School, we covered the end-zones with a large tarp and then revealed our design before kickoff!

Here's what it looked like in case you weren't at the game. [The speaker shows the end-zones on a projector screen in the room.]

It was such a fun project, and it's a good example of what goes on in the ASA. We want more creative people like you to join and come up with new projects we can do.

I hope you'll consider joining. Come up to me after class and ask any questions. Our first meeting of the year is on September 23 at 3 p.m. in Room 312. Thanks for listening!

Deeper Insight

Once you drop into story mode, you have the room's attention. People want to know, "What happens next?"

It's critical to walk in front of the audience with your story already selected. I recommend you practice the story out loud so you know how it sounds when you say it "live" in front of everyone.

Again, stories prove a point like nothing else. Your energy and enthusiasm about a student organization are great. That matters too.

But a concrete example of the inspiring work you do is the best way to make others excited and consider signing up.

HOW TO COMMUNICATE WITH A STATE OR NATIONAL OFFICER

As a leader in your school, you may need to communicate with a state or national officer in your organization. In those moments, communication skills are essential.

State and national officers are busy being students and leading the organization. Make sure your message is brief and focused.

Here's an example:

Subject line: [Reason or task; for instance, "Coordinating the regional conference"]

Hi [leader's first name],

Good morning/afternoon.

I'm [your first and last name], a/an/the [leadership title] with the [name of student organization] at [name of school] in [city and state; for instance, "Dallas, Texas"].

I'm reaching out [explain the purpose of the message right away; for instance, "to coordinate details about the opening ceremony for the regional conference on May 5 here at Acme High School"].

[Then, share relevant info or ask questions. Consider bullet points to make your message easy to follow. For instance:

"I have a few updates to pass along.

- We will have projector screens in all five breakout rooms if students have presentations to display.

- The ice cream social on Saturday will start at 5:30 p.m.

- The Saturday night party will happen in the school gym, but we need to have everyone out no later than 9:30 p.m."]

NOTES: Be specific when possible (ex: five breakout rooms, 9:30 p.m.)

[Then, wrap up the message; for instance, "Please let me know you saw these updates and pass along any info or questions."]

Thanks,

– Your first and last name

Email signature

Deeper Insight

It's important to start the email with a proper introduction so the state or national officer knows who you are, where you live and your role in the student organization back home.

Then, explain the reason for your email and give supporting details in an organized way (ex: bullet points).

The email recipient will appreciate your professional message.

HOW TO WRITE AN ARTICLE FOR A STUDENT OR COMMUNITY NEWSPAPER

You may need to write an article about a recent event or to highlight the successes of your organization.

It can be a challenge to start with a blank page and draft an article that's ready for a student or community newspaper.

The outline below will help you structure the article. The piece of writing can also serve as a blog post for a school or student organization website.

One note before you begin: What's the difference between an objective and subjective tone?

Objective: present the facts without opinion (example: The student walked to school).

Subjective: give an opinion (ex: The student walked **happily** to school).

In your article, use objective statements. If you provide a quote from someone, you share the person's opinion and the line is therefore subjective.

Article title: Explain what happened in one line to capture the reader's attention.

EXAMPLE:

Acme High School Senior Places Second in State Public Speaking Competition

Opening section: Reveal the recent success right away so you don't make the reader search around.

EXAMPLE:

> A senior at Acme High School won second place at the annual State Public Speaking Competition.
>
> The student, Annie Somers, delivered a five-minute speech on Thursday, May 7. A crowd of 250 people watched the competition's final round inside the auditorium at West High School in Anywhere, USA.
>
> *NOTE: Give readers the 4 Ws — who, what, when and where.*
>
> Somers's topic was "The importance of being multi-cultural in today's global economy." She discussed how, thanks to the digital age, people around the world are interconnected and need to find common ground to solve big challenges.

Second section: Explain why the recent success matters. Why should readers care?

EXAMPLE:

> Somers's victory is the first for Acme High School at the state competition since 2012. She is the fifth Acme student overall to place since the event began in 1993.

Third section: Provide a quote from a person close to the story or situation.

EXAMPLE:

> "I'm thrilled to come back to Acme High School with the second-place trophy," said Somers. "I worked hard all year to prepare, and I'm happy the judges felt I did a great job."

Fourth section: What are the next steps? Where does the "success" go from here?

EXAMPLE:

> Somers will place her trophy in the Champions Cabinet by the main office.
> The trophy will sit alongside other public speaking and debate titles won by
> Acme students over the years.

Fifth section: Call to action to engage people further.

EXAMPLE:

> All students who want to compete in public speaking competitions next
> year should attend the Public Speaking Club's upcoming meeting on Friday,
> May 15 in Room 324.

Deeper Insight

In the article, we:

1. Open with the main point or big news

2. Explain why the information matters

3. Share additional details like a quote

4. Let people know what happens next

5. Finish out with a clear call to action

The five-part outline will help you write an article that's clear and follows a logical progression.

HOW TO CONDUCT AN INTERVIEW WITH A BUSINESSPERSON

If you need to hold a Q&A (question and answer) session with someone in the business community, then you have an ideal opportunity to learn how to network too.

The best way to conduct a Q&A is to use your active listening skills and engage the person in a conversation. The typical approach is to write a list of questions and read them one by one.

For example:

1. What is your name?

2. What is your job?

3. What do you do in your job?

4. What are your hobbies?

Below, I will show you how to *listen* to the person's answers and use the responses to form your next question.

1. What's your name, and what do you do for a living?
My name is Cindy Lee, and I am vice president of Acme Bank.

NOTE: Now, notice how the next question draws upon the new information that Ms. Lee works for a bank.

2. Interesting. As vice president, what do you do for the bank?
I oversee all of our bank tellers and bank managers at 17 locations. It's a big job.

NOTE: See how Ms. Lee says, "It's a big job." Now is your chance to take the conversation deeper and learn why the position has so much responsibility.

3. Why is vice president such a big job?
Well, I am in charge of 132 bank tellers and 32 managers. Every day, my team handles more than $8 million of our customers' money.

NOTE: Eight million dollars is a huge number! Ask a question about keeping track of all that money.

4. Eight million — wow! Do you keep all of the money in a big safe?
No, the money is stored electronically in our computer systems.

NOTE: Dig deeper into the work.

5. So if I want your team to give me my money, what do I do?
You would walk into the bank or use an ATM, show proof of your identification and then receive your money either electronically into your account or in physical dollars and cents.

NOTE: Use your listening skills again. Ask about words or expressions you might not understand.

6. OK, I see. Also, what's an ATM?
ATM stands for automated teller machine and...

———

All right, let's recap.
When we began the section, I showed you a general Q&A with a businessperson:

1. What is your name?

2. What is your job?

3. What do you do in your job?

4. What are your hobbies?

When we use active listening skills, look how the questions change:

1. What's your name, and what do you do for a living?

2. Interesting. As vice president, what do you do for the bank?

3. Why is vice president such a big job?

4. Eight million — wow! Do you keep all of the money in a big safe?

5. So if I want your team to give me my money, what do I do?

6. OK, I see. Also, what's an ATM?

The first list is generic questions. The second list is a **conversation**.

How do you create the dialogue? Use eye contact, stay in the moment and think about ways to explore the person's world.

In fact, you won't hold a Q&A at all. You will conduct an interview and, in doing so, act like a true student leader.

HOW TO WRITE A PUBLIC STATEMENT

Not every communications scenario is upbeat and positive.

You may have situations where you, as a leader of your group, need to draft a public statement in response to an incident. You can send the statement out via email.

You might seek the advice of an advisor, educator or someone else more senior, but it's important to understand how to structure a sensitive message.

You could write in the first person (in the voice of a student leader) or as though the message comes from the organization as a whole.

In the example below, you will find the latter. First, here's the heading template for the public statement:

Organization's Address   Organization's Logo
                                [Day, Month and Year]

To Whom It May Concern,

First Section: Explain what has occurred

We, the members of [name of student organization; for instance, "Student Government Association (SGA) of Acme High School"], have a statement in response to [the situation; for instance, "the hurtful, racist graffiti spray-painted on the outside gymnasium walls the night of Tuesday, September 19"].

Second Section: Share your stance on the issue

[For instance: "The SGA does not condone such mean-spirited behavior that only hopes to divide our student body and school community. We know our school is at its best when all voices are heard, and we stand as one in the face of hate and bigotry."]

Third Section: Provide details on action items or next steps

[For instance: "The SGA invites Acme High School students to come together for a graffiti clean-up event and what we're calling the Rally Against Hate.

We will meet behind the gymnasium on Friday, September 22 at 3:15 p.m. Click here to RSVP so we can expect you."]

Fourth Section: Any last words

[For instance: "Acme High School is a place of inclusion, diversity and understanding. We will clean up the graffiti and continue to be a space for all students to grow and thrive."]

Sincerely,

– [Your first and last name] or [Name of the student organization]

Deeper Insight

The model above allows you to:

1. Explain what happened

2. Give your opinion

3. Share next steps

4. Provide a closing thought

The four-part outline makes sure the broader community hears your voice — or your organization's collective voice — during a difficult time.

BEST WRITING PRACTICES FOR E-NEWSLETTERS AND YEARBOOKS

What are the top strategies for e-newsletters and yearbooks?

In each case, you have the opportunity to learn valuable writing and communication skills that will help you in the college search, job market and in your career.

That's why I often say, "Write well, open doors!"

Here are the three biggest pointers to remember as you compose an e-newsletter for your student organization, build out the yearbook (physical or digital) or write something else altogether.

Context is everything

Always assume the reader knows nothing about your organization. That means, for example, you need to spell out abbreviations on first reference.

Example: "Congrats to the Acme High School Leadership Association (AHSLA) on winning first place at the state competition. AHSLA is a new club that started in the fall and…"

And with photos, provide all relevant information in the caption. Ask yourself, "Did I include the who, what, when, where and why?"

Example: The Acme High School Leadership Association (AHSLA) team **(WHO)** holds the first-place trophy at the state competition **(WHAT)** on Friday, October 26 **(WHEN)** in the Acme Hotel and Conference Center in Anytown, USA **(WHERE)**. The AHSLA team earned top honors for debate and extemporaneous speaking **(WHY)**.

Make headlines *pop*

For e-newsletters, avoid generic subject lines like "AHSLA E-Newsletter for May." Instead, catch the reader's eye and tease content from inside the e-newsletter.

For example: "AHSLA takes home top honors at state competition"

As for yearbooks and other student publications, infuse details into headlines. A headline like "Fun times at the AHS job fair" isn't likely to capture the reader's attention.

How about: "34 employers, 300+ students network at the first-ever AHS job fair"

Draw upon the details of the event or story to paint a picture for the audience. How many people came? How much money did you raise? What specifics do you have that make the experience special?

Find the emotion

At its best, good writing makes us feel a certain way. As you conduct interviews, don't be afraid to pose questions that capture the person's mood.

If you ask the teacher who organized the job fair a basic question, you will receive a generic answer.

Question: "Did you think the job fair was a success?"

Answer: "Yes, I am happy with how the day turned out. We had a lot of employers attend and share their businesses with our students."

Now, use "Why?" to pull the emotion out of the person.

Question: "Why was it important to organize the mock job fair?"

Answer: "Too often, I see students struggle when they talk with employers. They don't know what to say or how to hold conversations. I hope the AHS job fair gave our students practical skills they can carry with them to the next job fair or actual job interview."

Always remember to ask the person, "Why?"

That's where you will find the emotion in the interview.

SOCIAL MEDIA: CAPITALIZATION AND APOSTROPHES

The two biggest mistakes I see students and adults make on social media focus on capitalization and apostrophes.

1. Capitalization: we think way too many words are upper case

"We're so excited to Welcome Everyone to our Kickoff Meeting on Tuesday Night!"

Only two words in the above sentence should be capitalized. Do you know what they are?

▶ We're (the first word in the sentence)

▸ Tuesday (proper noun)

Every other word is lower case.

"We're so excited to welcome everyone to our kickoff meeting on Tuesday night!"

Unless the word is a proper noun, do not capitalize. I know sometimes words *feel* important ("Welcome Everyone"), but they do not receive the uppercase treatment.

Examples of proper nouns:

▸ Name of your school (Acme High School)

▸ Name of your organization (National Honor Society)

▸ Name of an event (2019 Spring Conclave)

▸ Name of a piece of technology (Google Chromebook)

2. Apostrophes: we think plural words need an apostrophe

"We expect to have more than 200 student's at the rally."

Incorrect. We use an apostrophe to show possession.

"I took the student's backpack by mistake."

When we use plural nouns, there's no need for apostrophes. Add the "s" and leave it at that (ex: "We expect to have more than 200 students at the rally").

As you compose social media content, keep your capitalization to a minimum and leave apostrophes out of the mix with respect to plural words.

Thank-you notes

HANDWRITTEN NOTE BEST PRACTICES

How to send a handwritten note:

▸ If the note opens vertically, write on the bottom half. Horizontally, use the right side.

▸ Put the day's date (month and day as in "3/27" or "March 27") in the upper right.

- The projects could be:
  - ○ Class assignment in which multiple students have responsibilities
  - ○ Initiative related to a club or organization
  - ○ Upcoming event that has several logistical pieces to manage
- Discuss the importance of the word "please" so the leader's tone is polite.
- Encourage the students to be specific in their wording. Note how, on page 55 of *Wait, How Do I Lead My Team?*, the line reads:
  - ○ "Margo, the senior VP at Acme, asked to see the latest mock-ups by today at 4 p.m."
    - ■ "latest mock-ups" is more specific than "Are you done with it yet?" Tell students to avoid pronouns and employ proper nouns so the message is clear.

Question to ask the group:
- Which people on your team received the follow-up email? What are the tasks they need to do?
- What kind of specific language did you use in your email (ex: "latest mock-ups")?
- How did you incorporate the word "please" so your tone is courteous and respectful?

Classroom Activity: How to Request Keynote Speakers or Workshop Presenters

As a leader, it may be your responsibility to develop the programming for an upcoming conference or event. In that case, you will need to write emails to special guests like potential keynote speakers or workshop presenters.

Each time, make your message personal and authentic to stand the best chance at a response.

Instructions:

Step 1: By yourself or as a group, read pages 159–161 of *Wait, How Do I Lead My Team?* to understand the proper way to invite keynote speakers or workshop presenters.

Step 2: Think about an upcoming event where you may need to invite significant people. By yourself or as part of a team, discuss at least one person you want to invite as a keynote speaker or workshop presenter. Why do you hope that person can attend? What makes him/her special?

Step 3: Write your email and follow the template on pages 159–161. Note how you should include basic details about the event (example on page 159: "Rise Up National Conference over the weekend of October 5–7 in Kansas City, Missouri") and one detail about the person's career that stands out (example on page 160: "I…enjoyed your blog, especially your post about entrepreneurship tips").

Step 4: Read your email out loud to look for any typos or awkward phrases.

Be ready to share the email with the instructor or your group.

Teacher Notes: How to Request Keynote Speakers or Workshop Presenters
Estimated class time: 20–30 minutes

Leaders are the faces of your organization and ambassadors that spread the message in all directions. That means leaders should be counted on to reach out and invite keynote speakers and workshop presenters for upcoming events.

It's impressive when a student leader writes a professional email to seek the participation of a speaker or presenter. The activity will guide students to write such an email.

Learning outcome:
A well-written email will command the respect of potential speakers and teach students how to build relationships with their words.

Notes for the exercise:

- It's best for students to draw upon their own projects to learn how to write the thank-you note. The projects could be:
    - Conference or competition
    - Career fair or other gathering in which employers attended and had roles (ex: stage a booth)
- The email template on pages 159–161 stresses two points: context and research. Make sure students understand the importance of both elements.
    - **Context:** Note how the email template provides a brief description of the student organization and basic details of the event.
        - "the leading student organization in the U.S. for jobs in farming and agriculture"
        - "Rise Up National Conference over the weekend of October 5–7 in Kansas City, Missouri"
            - Ask students: Why does the email recipient need both pieces of information? Why do we need to provide general information about who we are and what we do before the person can make the decision to attend?
    - **Research:** Note how the email template includes research on the speaker's career.
        - "I spent time on your website and enjoyed your blog, especially your post about entrepreneurship tips for people in the farming industry."
            - Have students visit the website for the speaker or the speaker's company and read a blog post or other web page they find interesting. Pages like Blog, News, Latest News or Press Releases are great places to look.
            - Ask students: What did you read and why do you find the information interesting? How can you incorporate what you found similar to the template on pages 159–160? Why is it smart to show you have done homework on the person and respect what he/she does?

Question to ask the group:

- Who do you plan to invite as a keynote speaker or workshop presenter?
- Why is it important to make every request for speakers or presenters customized for the recipient?
- How would it make you feel if people took the time to learn about *your* background and talents before they reached out to you?

Conclusion

In the book's introduction, I described leadership as life under a microscope.

As a leader, your actions (the good, bad and ugly) are magnified for all around you to see.

For people in leadership roles, that reality shouldn't be a reason to run and hide under your desk. It's a daily opportunity to shine because of how *well* you write, speak and engage with others.

That means take an extra three minutes to edit an email to your staff. Maintain the proper tone and structure the information in a logical way.

Think hard about an upcoming presentation. How can you keep your pitch brief and abide by the "less is more" approach? What story can you tell to have the audience waiting on your every word?

Leadership is more than a title outside an office door or affixed to an online profile. It's how we carry ourselves in the micro-moments that make a career — the untold thousands of emails, staff meetings, client engagements, presentations and one-off conversations in the break room.

It's every single day of our professional lives. No breaks. No do-overs.

The microscope is on.

What's your next move?

Thank-yous

In 2012, I began a personal blog as a way to stoke my writing hobby.

Seven years later, I have now published my third book.

I could never have predicted in 2012 that a blog would turn into a book series on practical writing instruction. It's been an organic process where one idea yields the next. Nothing forced or rushed.

Still, that's seven years of sacrifice — and not only from me. Thank you to my wife, Shikma, for understanding why I need to sit at my computer a little each day and fill all these pages with words. You know better than anyone each book is part of a bigger journey for my career and our family.

I also owe a debt of gratitude to my parents, Joel and Sara Jo, who double as my colleagues at our family's public relations firm, Rubin Communications Group. From both of you, I have learned the technical side of communication and how to treat people the right way. To me, that's the entire leadership equation.

Many thanks to the readers of my blog, THE TEMPLATE, who provided spot-on suggestions for communication challenges they face as leaders. Special shout-out to Merav Fine Braun for taking me inside the world of non-profit management.

I want my books to provide solutions to actual, on-the-ground situations. Everyone's feedback and insights made sure of that.

And how could I forget? Thanks to all the leaders in my life — the great ones and the ones who, shall we say, need sensitivity training.

Lessons come in all shapes and sizes. We are who we are because of the people on our path. I wouldn't trade a single person.

As for you…

Go forth and manage people in a way only you can.

As you do, remember the power of our words to raise people up or lower them down.

"Leader" is the role you are meant to play.

Curtains up.

Index